Glory, Valor & Sacrifice

MICHIGAN SITES SIGNIFICANT TO THE CIVIL WAR

Nolan Medere in front of Civil War monument at Brookside Cemetery, Tecumseh. Photo by Ron Medere

Compiled by DAVID INGALL & KARIN RISKO

Published by

HOMETOWN HISTORY TOURS

Grosse Ile, MI

Copyright ©2012 by David Ingall and Karin Risko

ISBN: 978-0615-56574-3

Enjoy discovering Civil War Michigan! David Ingall

To Donna, Yours in History, Karin Risko "2012"

CONTENTS

Acknowledgements

Steve Alexander, Allen Barksdale, Thomas Berlucchi, Marty Bertera, Jack Dempsey, David Finney, Kirt Gross, Gail Hershenzon, David Jamroz, Rod Leighton, Shawna Mazur, Mark McPherson, Bill Munday, Phyllis Rickard and Don Schwarck for sharing not only your expertise but your passion for history. A special thank you to David Finney, Elizabeth Ingall, Regina Manning and Charmaine Wawrzyniec for your proofreading and editing assistance; Gary Wlosinski for your support and encouragement.

Dedicated to Colonel Thornton Brodhead

This guidebook is dedicated to Colonel Thornton Fleming Brodhead, a prominent publisher and public servant who once resided on Grosse Ile. This family man, who valiantly fought to save the Nation he so loved and died doing so, was mortally wounded at the Second Battle of Bull Run. From his deathbed, he penned this poignant farewell letter to his wife and six children:

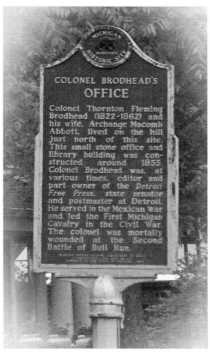

"Two bullets have gone through my Chest, and directly through the lung. I suffer little now, but at first the pain was acute. I have won the Soldier's fate. I hope that from heaven I may see the glorious old Flag waive again over the individual Union I have loved so well. Farewell wife and Babes and Friends. We shall meet again."

– *Your loving Thornton*

A state marker identifies the site of Colonel Brodhead's former East River study. From the street, you can see the exterior walls of the structure which is located on private property.

Foreword

GAR plot at Elmwood Cemetery

*B*ruce Catton, the nation's foremost Civil War historian and Michigan's own, wrote how the soldiers and sailors who served during the Civil War contended desperately with a fate that was almost more than they could cope with. Abraham Lincoln predicted that the world could not, would not, forget what they did.

Michigan sent some 90,000 troops off to war, defending the American Union and ending the great evil of slavery in America. One of every six never came home alive. Many who returned had suffered wounds, illness, and imprisonment. Their sacrifice was a great and bloody one.

The Michiganders who stepped up during our country's greatest crisis came from all over Michigan, from city and farm and far-flung posts, where they were already serving. They were as young as teenagers and as old as the late stages of life. They were Native American, African American, Irish American, and just about every other kind of American. Some in uniform were female; those women who did not wear Union blue kept up the family, farm, or store, went close to the front to provide necessary support and helped in overmatched hospital wards.

Their service was made possible by a Michigan electorate that kept raising up leaders who would not tolerate two American nations to exist on the same continent.

In many respects, the issues that confronted Michigan a century and a half ago still challenge us - chief among them whether we are a society of equal opportunity. The Civil War remains relevant.

It is for us to remember what they did, how they contended with a desperate fate, and how they overcame. It is for us to comprehend the rebirth of American freedom that should resonate yet today and ever down through the corridors of time.

This guidebook is an invaluable resource for discovering Civil War heritage. It documents history that should never be forgotten. There is nothing comparable, whether career historian or casual tourist, to seeing such monuments and locations up close and personal.

Jack Dempsey – *Chairman of the Michigan Civil War Sesquicentennial Committee*

Jack Dempsey, author of Michigan and the Civil War: A Great and Bloody Sacrifice, is a partner at the law firm of Dickinson Wright PLLC in Ann Arbor, Michigan. Born in Detroit, Mr. Dempsey received his undergraduate degree in political science from Michigan State University and his law degree from George Washington University. He and his wife Suzzanne reside in Plymouth.

In addition to serving as chairman of the Michigan Civil War Sesquicentennial Committee, Mr. Dempsey is vice-president of the Michigan Historical Commission, chairman of the Michigan History Foundation, member of the Ann Arbor Civil War Roundtable, color bearer for the Civil War Trust, and publisher of the popular blog, Michigan and the Civil War.

Introduction

Prominent Detroit businessman and Underground Railroad conductor George DeBaptist
points across the Detroit River to Canada, the end of the treacherous journey to freedom.

Thank God for Michigan! It is believed President Abraham Lincoln uttered those words when the 1st Michigan Infantry arrived in Washington D.C., shortly after the president's declaration of war. The 1st Michigan was the first western unit to answer his call.

More than 90,000 Michigan residents, nearly 23 percent of the state's male population in 1860, served the Union during the American Civil War. Nearly 15,000 made the ultimate sacrifice by giving their lives for the Union cause. These people fought hard and sacrificed much. Their actions significantly contributed to the outcome we enjoy today – a united nation - the United States of America. The people of Michigan should know this and be proud.

Glory, Valor & Sacrifice: Michigan Sites Significant to the Civil War brings the war home by identifying the local people (as well as places and events) whose efforts helped preserve the Union, and thereby, shaped our Nation's history.

This guidebook is NOT the definitive book on Michigan's role in the Civil War. There is much more to be told. Rather, this guidebook is meant to be a catalyst that ignites reader interest in further exploring the huge role Michigan played in the Civil War. Hometown History Tours recommends guidebook users seek out and read the various publications listed on the resource page found at the end of the guide for more in-depth coverage of the various sites featured.

Michigan State University, Central Michigan University and Western Michigan University archives contain Civil War letters, diaries and photographs, as do the archives at many state colleges, county museums and local libraries.

Other resources worth exploring include the Detroit Historical Museum, Sloan Museum in Flint, Michigan State University Museum in East Lansing and Washtenaw County Historical Museum in Ann Arbor. All have substantial Civil War collections, but do not display them on a continual basis.

Every attempt has been made to publish the most current information. Please contact sites in advance to verify hours of operation and fee schedules.

SOUTHEAST MICHIGAN

I

When it comes to unearthing Civil War history, southeast Michigan usually does not come to mind. Far removed from the major battlefields and action, people underestimate the role its citizens played in this conflict. A large northern city, Detroit was instrumental in recruiting and organizing troops, including the 1st Michigan Infantry, who were the first western regiment to answer Lincoln's call for troops, eliciting his famous response: "Thank God for Michigan!"

Several highly-acclaimed regiments originated from this region and many individuals earned accolades for bravery and meritorious service. Off the battlefield, outspoken activists influenced public opinion, while lawmakers brandished pens and authored major legislation that shaped national policy.

One of America's most coveted artifacts, the original black walnut rocking chair, where **President Abraham Lincoln**, our nation's 16th president, was seated when assassinated, is displayed right here in southeast Michigan at The Henry Ford.

On April 14, 1865, the President and First Lady Mary Todd Lincoln attended a performance of the play *Our American Cousin* at the famed Ford's Theatre in Washington, D.C., when actor and Confederate sympathizer John Wilkes Booth shot and killed him. Ranked among the greatest presidents in United States history, Lincoln successfully led the nation through the American Civil War, our country's greatest internal crisis. He preserved the Union and abolished, forever, the repugnant institution of slavery. The theater chair, a remnant from our history's darkest hour, was put up for auction in 1929. Agents representing automobile mogul Henry Ford purchased this priceless artifact for $2,400.

While many argue the Civil War was about states' rights not slavery, and President Lincoln never intended to free the slaves, slavery was the issue that divided the nation and caused the Confederate states to secede. With its proximity to Canada, southeast Michigan played an important role in the secretive network known as the Underground Railroad. Fervent abolitionists risked their own lives to help thousands of freedom seekers make this long and treacherous journey through the lower portion of our state and on to freedom.

While most Civil War era structures have long been replaced by modern construction, some period residences, churches and commercial buildings still exist. From Jonesville, to Pontiac, to the historic island of Grosse Ile, you will find private residences or public museums occupying the beautiful homes that once belonged to prominent people of this period.

A Civil War tour of southeast Michigan would not be complete without a visit to Monroe County, the gateway to Michigan's Civil War history. The city of Monroe is the adopted hometown of **General George Armstrong Custer**, one of the youngest Union generals to serve in the Civil War. Commander of the acclaimed Michigan Cavalry Brigade, Custer rallied his men with the famous battle cry: "C'mon you Wolverines!"

The Michigan Cavalry Brigade thwarted numerous Confederate advances and participated in many critical campaigns that helped secure Union victory. While Custer's men captured numerous Confederate battle flags, they never lost a color.

In a charge led by Custer himself, the Michigan Cavalry Brigade forced the retreat of the once invincible General James Ewell Brown "Jeb" Stuart and his Confederate Cavalry at Gettysburg in what is often called "the cavalry battle that saved the Union."

At the Battle of Yellow Tavern, a member of Custer's brigade, Private John A. Huff, delivered a huge blow to the Confederacy when he shot and mortally wounded General Stuart. Near the end of the war, it was the 3rd Cavalry Division under Custer's command, which blocked the retreat of Confederate General Robert E. Lee's forces, resulting in Lee's subsequent surrender.

Southeast Michigan offers numerous opportunities for history buffs to learn firsthand about our Nation's greatest internal crisis and the people from this region who valiantly rose to meet this threat to our national security. Here you will find repositories rich in primary resources such as letters, diaries, and documents; first rate museums and exhibits; exquisite displays of sculpture and architecture that utilize artistic expression as a means to immortalize yesterday's heroes; a distinctive 83-acre fort that serves as a rich cultural and military history institute, along with the many beautiful and peaceful preserves that serve as the final resting places for those who served and sacrificed on behalf of our Nation and created the America we celebrate today.

Adrian

LAURA SMITH HAVILAND STATUE

Church and South Main Streets

This monument once stood on the grounds of the former Adrian City Hall dedicated to suffragette, social reformer, abolitionist, Underground Railroad conductor, and Civil War nurse **Laura Smith Haviland**, also known as Aunt Laura. Originally from Canada, Haviland, a Quaker, founded the State Public School for Dependent Children in Coldwater and co-founded the Raisin Institute of Learning, one of the first schools in the United States to allow black students to attend. The Raisin Institute and Haviland farm served as stops on the Underground Railroad. Haviland's abolitionist activities were so successful that one Southern slave owner posted a $3,000 bounty to anyone willing to kidnap or murder her on his behalf.

When the Civil War ended, Haviland toured abandoned plantations and collected the chains, irons, restraints, and other implements which had been used to keep slaves in line. She transported these items north and exhibited them during her lectures to help whites understand the travesty freed blacks had been subjected to as slaves.

When the Adrian City Hall was torn down in 2010, Haviland's statue was packed away. It will be relocated at Church and Main next to the Lenawee County Historical Museum.

RAISIN VALLEY FRIENDS MEETING HOUSE | RAISIN VALLEY CEMETERY

West Valley Rd. | *(west of North Adrian Highway / M-52)*

The Raisin Valley Cemetery is the site of the Haviland family burial plot. Adjacent to the cemetery is the Raisin Valley Friends Meeting House where Laura Haviland's father once served as Pastor.

CHANDLER FAMILY CEMETERY/HAZLEBANK

Breckel Highway near East Valley Road | *Raisin Township* | *private property*

Elizabeth Margaret Chandler, a noted Quaker poet and abolitionist, lived near Laura Haviland. The two neighbors and friends co-founded the Logan Female Anti-Slavery Society in 1832. In 1830, Ms. Chandler moved with her aunt from Philadelphia, Pennsylvania to a farm purchased by her brother, Thomas, on the outskirts of Tecumseh. They called the farm Hazlebank. Already a nationally published author, Ms. Chandler continued to publish poems and writings that not only depicted the injustice of slavery and demanded better treatment for Native Americans and the emancipation of slaves, but encouraged women to be the agents of change.

FOURTH MICHIGAN INFANTRY TRAINING SITE

110 South Madison

Marker at Adrian College's North Hall denotes Camp Williams, site of the 4th Michigan Infantry training camp.

OAKWOOD CEMETERY

1001 Oakwood Avenue

Colonel Dwight A. Woodbury of the 4th Michigan Infantry and **Brigadier General William Humphrey** are buried here. Colonel Woodbury was killed at the Battle of Malvern Hill on July 1, 1862.

General Humphrey, twice wounded at the Battle of Spotsylvania, served in numerous major battles. At Cold Harbor he was charged with maintaining the picket line in front of the enemy as General Grant's army withdrew to the

south side of the James River. After the war, General Humphrey became a newspaper editor, manufacturer, Auditor General of Michigan, Jackson State Prison Warden, and Adrian Postmaster.

Private George Post of Company I, 7th U.S. Cavalry was killed June 25, 1876, along with General George Armstrong Custer, on "Last Stand Hill" at the Battle of Little Big Horn in Montana. His memorial stone is inscribed with the words: "Killed in Custer massacre." His remains lay on the battlefield.

LENAWEE COUNTY HISTORICAL SOCIETY MUSEUM

110 East Church Street | *(517) 265-6071*

Museum features Civil War exhibit and artifacts of interest.

MONUMENT PARK

Center Street between Maumee and Church

Adrian's Civil War monument was dedicated in 1870. The marble column used in the monument dates back further in American history to 1799 when it stood in front of the Bank of Pennsylvania in Philadelphia.

Ann Arbor

UNIVERSITY OF MICHIGAN CAMPUS

Alumni Memorial Hall | *525 South State Street* | *(734) 764-0395*

Approximately 1,500 students from the University of Michigan went to war. Over 100 died. A plaque honoring the 20th Michigan Infantry hangs in Alumni Memorial Hall, now the university's Museum of Art. The alumni association dedicated the hall to university students who died in both the Civil and Spanish American Wars.

Bentley Historical Library | *1150 Beal Avenue* | *(734) 764-3482*

The Bentley Historical Library covers all periods of Michigan history. The library has an extensive collection of items relating to Michigan and the Civil War including primary sources, books, newspapers, documents, etc.

William L. Clements Library | *909 South University Avenue* | *(734) 764-2347*

This library has an impressive non-Michigan related Civil War collection.

SIGNAL OF LIBERTY

1000 block of Broadway | *building no longer exists*

In April 1841, abolitionists **Theodore Foster** and **Reverend Guy Beckley** launched the *Signal of Liberty*, the state's most prominent anti-slavery newspaper, above the mercantile shop belonging to Reverend Beckley's brother Josiah. The weekly publication featured stories designed to arouse sympathy and gain support for the abolitionist agenda, which was to end slavery in America. The *Signal of Liberty* is digitized and can now be accessed online.

REVEREND GUY BECKLEY HOUSE

1425 Pontiac Trail | *private residence*

Reverend Guy Beckley, publisher of the abolitionist newspaper *The Signal of Liberty*, resided here with his family. It is believed Reverend Beckley's home served as a station on the secretive network known as the Underground Railroad.

AFRICAN AMERICAN CULTURAL AND HISTORICAL MUSEUM

3261 Lohr Road

The African American Cultural and Historical Museum was founded in 1993 to house, catalogue, preserve, display, and maintain a collection of artifacts, art, papers, books, photographs, and other materials pertaining to the history and culture of African Americans in Washtenaw County. Programming includes Underground Railroad tours which illustrate the important role the cities of Ann Arbor and Ypsilanti played in this secret network as freedom seekers made their way to Detroit.

The administrative building is currently located in the David R. Byrd Center, an 1830s farmhouse, that was restored by the late David. R. Byrd, a prominent African American architect. The beautiful chapel adjacent to the museum was also built by Mr. Byrd. A legacy campaign is underway by the organization to occupy another historic home located at 1528 Pontiac Trail.

FAIRVIEW CEMETERY

1401 Wright Street

A Civil War monument, featuring an eagle on top, graces the grounds of this cemetery.

FOREST HILL CEMETERY

415 South Observatory Street

Two Medal of Honor recipients are buried here. **Sergeant Conrad Noll**, of the 20th Michigan Infantry, Company D, received his medal for exemplifying courage when he saved the regiment's colors at Spotsylvania on May 12, 1864. **Sergeant Joseph B. Kemp**, of the 5th Michigan Infantry, Company D, earned his medal for capturing the flag of the 31st North Carolina Infantry at the Battle of the Wilderness on May 6, 1864.

Colonel Norvell E. Welch, of the 16th Michigan Infantry, is also buried here. Welch was killed at the Battle of Peeble's Farm, Virginia, on September 30, 1864.

A Civil War soldier monument, at parade rest, honors soldiers and sailors from Washtenaw County.

St. Thomas Cemetery
300 Sunset Road

Sergeant Patrick Irwin, of the 14th Michigan Infantry, Company H, is interred here. Sergeant Irwin was awarded the Medal of Honor for capturing a Confederate general and his command at Greensboro, Georgia on September 1, 1864.

Armada
Willow Grove Cemetery
Armada Ridge Road

Willow Grove Cemetery is the final resting place of **Private John A. Huff**, a member of Company E, 5th Michigan Cavalry. On May 11, 1864, during the Battle of Yellow Tavern, Virginia, Private Huff shot and mortally wounded Confederate Major General Jeb Stuart with a .44 caliber colt revolver when the general and his staff rode within a close distance of Huff and portions of the 5th Michigan. General Stuart's death was a monumental loss to the Confederacy. Unfortunately, Huff would also die on June 23, 1864 due to complications from a head wound received during the Battle of Hawes Shop, Virginia, on May 28, 1864.

Blissfield
Pleasant View Cemetery
U.S. 223 and High Street

Columbiad cannon, placed by the local GAR Scott Post #43, is located here.

Ogden Zion Cemetery
Crockett Highway and East Horton Road

GAR monument, paying tribute to our fallen heroes, is located in cemetery. Here rests **Corporal Addison J. Hodges** of Company B, 47th Ohio Infantry. He was awarded the Medal of Honor for action at Vicksburg, Mississippi on May 3, 1863 for being a member of a party that volunteered and attempted to run the enemy's batteries with a steam tug and two barges loaded with explosives.

Bloomfield Hills
Christ Church Cranbrook
470 Church Street

A statue of a beardless **Abraham Lincoln** stands on the north side of the church which was built in 1928.

Brooklyn
Walker Tavern Historic Site
13320 M-50

Built in 1832, the Walker Tavern is a pre-Civil War building that provided respite to early visitors and settlers traveling to and from Michigan via stagecoach and pioneer wagon. Conveniently located at Cambridge Junction, where the Monroe Pike and Chicago Road met, the tavern thrived until the 1860s when railroads replaced stagecoaches and wagons as the main mode of transportation.

Massachusetts lawyer, senator, and three-time presidential candidate **Daniel Webster** once stayed there. Webster wanted to preserve the Union, but avoid a civil war. On March 7, 1850, this great orator delivered a speech that supported the Compromise of 1850. A hotly contested component of this compromise was the Fugitive Slave Law of 1850, which required the federal government to recapture and return runaway slaves. Webster's "Seventh of March" speech enraged abolitionists who likened him to Lucifer. Webster never recovered from the loss of popularity that resulted from the delivery of this speech.

The Chicago Road, now called US-12, stretches across the lower portion of Michigan between New Buffalo on the west side of the state and Detroit on the east side of the state. It is also designated as Iron Brigade Memorial Highway.

Dearborn

THE HENRY FORD | THE LINCOLN CHAIR

20900 Oakwood Blvd. | *(313) 982-6001* | *admission fee*

President Lincoln tried desperately to hold the country together during the Civil War. He ultimately realized that declaring an end to slavery was the only means of preserving the Union.

One section of the exhibit features moral reformers, including radical abolitionists, as they protest the nation's failure to live up to its foundational principles—set forth in the Declaration of Independence—with its continued acceptance of slavery. A rare grouping of artifacts relating to slavery, including a whip, shackles, and neck collar paint a graphic picture of this once acceptable institution.

In another setting, exhibit goers "meet" the people involved in the 1851 Christiana Revolt (Pennsylvania) where a slave owner pursuing four runaways was stymied by sympathetic whites and blacks and lost his life in the resulting confrontation. An audio program draws on the writings of Frederick Douglass illustrating the impact of this influential communicator in shaping the public opinion at the time.

How did Abraham Lincoln come to grips with issues that split the nation? Through artifacts, images, and interactive panels, visitors can explore Lincoln's background, assess his leadership qualities, and understand the evolution of his political views, starting with the highly publicized debates with Stephen Douglas.

The Gettysburg Address, Lincoln's key speech, is dramatized in a short, audio program. Photographs, engravings, and lithographs illustrating key battles of the Civil War accompany this exhibit. An original copy of the 13th Amendment (which abolished slavery) bearing Lincoln's signature, as well as those of 148 members of Congress, is also available for viewing.

The centerpiece of the *With Liberty and Justice for All* exhibit is the actual chair from the Ford's Theatre where Lincoln was seated when assassinated. The chair sits in a special case along with a theater handbill from the evening's performance. Period mourning items complete the vignette.

With Liberty and Justice for All explores the defining moments of American freedom from the revolution through the civil rights movement.

GREENFIELD VILLAGE | THE LOGAN COUNTY COURTHOUSE

20900 Oakwood Blvd. | *(313) 982-6001* | *admission fee*

The Logan County Courthouse at Greenfield Village is the actual Pottsville, Illinois building where a young lawyer and rising Whig politician named **Abraham Lincoln** came to argue cases before a judge on behalf of his clients.

Other Civil War era buildings can be found inside Greenfield Village, including the Susquehanna Plantation, once located in the Tidewater region of Maryland.

DEARBORN HISTORICAL MUSEUM | COMMANDANT'S QUARTERS

21950 Michigan Ave. | *(313) 565-0844*

The two principal buildings that make up the Dearborn Historical Museum were part of the United States Detroit Arsenal, an 11 building, 360-foot square, walled compound, built in 1833 and located in what was then called Dearbornville. The Detroit Arsenal served as an occasional training and recruiting center during the Civil War.

Today, the museum displays a few artifacts significant to the Civil War era. The 1st Michigan Cavalry Battle Flag of Company E is displayed in the basement of the Commandant's Quarters. The First Michigan Cavalry mustered in at Camp Lyons, Hamtramck, under **Colonel Thornton Fleming Brodhead** and later served with distinction under General George Armstrong Custer. The First Michigan Cavalry's battle flag was proudly carried and protected by **Thomas Henry Sheppard** throughout the war. In total, the flag survived 13 major battles, over one hundred skirmishes, 72 bullet holes, and capture.

One interesting incident includes the battle flag being fired upon by southern civilian women. A front page article in the June 12, 1889 issue of the *Detroit Free Press* retold the story as follows:

"It was fresh in color and sound of texture when, by order of Colonel Brodhead it was hung from the window of the Court House at Charleston near Harpers Ferry; but the women of the town made it a target and when, with the movement of the regiment it was taken in, there were five bullet holes to show the feeling of the irreconcilables in petticoats!"

Color Bearer Sergeant Thomas Henry Sheppard led the First Michigan through several major battles. At Gettysburg, a member of Confederate General Jeb Stuart's cavalry slashed him with a saber and struck him from his horse. Sheppard sustained injuries to his shoulder and ankle and was unable to flee to safety.

Knowing he would be captured, Sheppard ripped the flag from its staff and concealed it under his clothing. Miraculously, both Sheppard and the flag endured and survived 505 days of imprisonment under the most wretched conditions at Libby Prison, Belle Isle and the infamous Andersonville Prison.

Detroit

WOODMERE CEMETERY

9400 W. Fort St. | *(313) 841-0188*

Woodmere Cemetery is the final resting place for many Civil War soldiers, notable public figures, business owners and politicians.

Several members of the 4th Michigan Infantry are buried here. This regiment fought in numerous major campaigns with the Army of the Potomac and is one of the few to have lost more men in battle than to disease.

Michael Vreeland served in the 4th Michigan Infantry and is buried in Lot 370. A farmer living in Brownstown, Vreeland enlisted in 1861 and was promoted to brigadier general. The Vreeland family played a prominent role in settling the area of southeast Michigan known as Downriver and more specifically the city of Flat Rock. A major area road is named Vreeland in honor of the family.

In 1991, members of a reenacting group representing this regiment restored Vreeland's monument and added a commemorative plaque that reads: "Gravely wounded in the 'Wheatfield' Gettysburg, Pa. July 2, 1863."

Several members of the 4th Michigan Cavalry are also buried here. This regiment fought with distinction in numerous campaigns and is best known as being part of the famous Minty's Saber Brigade and for capturing the president of the Confederate States of America, Jefferson Davis, as he attempted to flee at the end of the war.

AMERICA'S FIRST SOFT DRINK FOUNDED BY CIVIL WAR VETERAN - Hires Root Beer and Vernors Ginger Ale both claim the title of first American soft drink. Many argue, however, that Hires was just another root beer while Vernors was distinctly different from other ginger beers or ginger ales. That's why Vernors is considered the oldest surviving American soft drink still served today. James Vernor enlisted in the famed 4th Michigan Cavalry, initially serving as a hospital steward and was later promoted to second lieutenant.

Prominent Detroit pharmacist and businessman **James Vernor**, who is known locally for inventing Vernor's Ginger Ale, was a member of this acclaimed regiment. Vernor, who enlisted in the 4th Michigan Cavalry as a hospital steward at age 19, lost his right eye while in service to his country. He was also captured during battle, but later rescued.

Originally from New York, Vernor and his family moved to Detroit when he was a young boy. According to local lore, Vernor began experimenting with a formula for ginger ale while working as a clerk at Detroit's Higby & Sterns Drug Store, prior to joining the 4th Michigan. When Vernor set off for war, he left his experimental concoction behind, stored in an oak barrel. Upon his return home to Detroit after being discharged from the service in July 1865, Vernor discovered the secret ingredients he left behind had aged into a delicious beverage which he proudly dubbed Vernor's Ginger Ale.

Although not made in Detroit anymore, Vernors Ginger Ale (apostrophe dropped in later years by the company) is part of Plano, Texas-based Dr. Pepper Snapple Group, Inc. Due to its continuous production, Vernors Ginger Ale enjoys the distinction of being America's oldest surviving soft drink still served today.

Jacob Siegel, a successful Detroit merchant and founder of the American Lady Corset Company, is buried in the family mausoleum along with his cousin, Benjamin, another prominent Detroit clothier. Jacob Siegel was in attendance at Ford's Theatre on the same evening President Lincoln was assassinated. Innkeeper and abolitionist **Seymour Finney** is buried at Woodmere as well.

In 1896, Woodmere Cemetery agreed to provide burial space for soldiers and sold 10,000 square feet of property to the government. From November to December of that year, 156 bodies were reinterred from Fort Wayne's decaying cemetery to Woodmere. Fort Wayne's cemetery records were in such disarray that 34 of the 156 bodies moved were unknown. A flagpole divides the G.A.R. section on the left from the U.S. Army section on the right. The cemetery offers an eight page publication entitled *Michigan Notables and Civil War Soldiers Buried at Woodmere Cemetery* in addition to the book by author Gail D. Hershenzon, *Detroit's Woodmere Cemetery*.

MOUNT ELLIOTT CEMETERY

1701 Mount Elliot St.

Buried here is Medal of Honor recipient **Patrick Colbert**, a sailor aboard the USS Commodore during the capture of Plymouth, North Carolina on October 31, 1864. As captain of the forward pivot gun, Private Colbert remained at his post - even though he sustained severe injuries - and battled heavy enemy fire until the action subsided.

HISTORIC FORT WAYNE

6325 West Jefferson Ave. | *(313) 224-6385* | *parking fee*

Detroit's Historic Fort Wayne is the only American fort still standing with its original star fort configuration intact. Fort Wayne was built in the 1840s as a means to protect the northern border of the United States from British attack. By 1849, the British threat diminished and the fort's importance subsided.

When the Civil War broke out, Fort Wayne was utilized heavily as a recruiting and training station for Michigan troops. Thousands of soldiers passed through as they headed off to battle. The fort underwent massive construction changes during this time. For national security purposes, the original earthen fortifications were replaced by brick and concrete walls.

While the fort was utilized through the Vietnam era and expanded numerous times to meet military needs of the time, Civil War enthusiasts can walk through a portion of the fort that hasn't changed. Built between 1842 and 1849, the Federal-style, limestone troop barracks that housed soldiers during the Civil War still stands. A room has been recreated to depict the cramped conditions enlistees endured. A long list of rules billeting soldiers had to follow back then is posted on the wall.

Montgomery Miegs, who designed Fort Wayne and supervised its construction, later laid the foundation for what is now known as Arlington National Cemetery. As U.S. Quartermaster General during the Civil War, Miegs, who was a former West Point classmate of Confederate General Robert E. Lee, proposed the confiscation of 200 acres from the Lee estate to be used to bury Union casualties of war.

Fort Wayne may have been one of the final stops on the Underground Railroad prior to the Civil War. The fort's location at one of the narrowest parts of the Detroit River would have made it an excellent crossing point,

and, for many years, the fort was abandoned except for a lone security guard who resided on the property. References have been made in a few escaped slave narratives of departures from a wharf in Springwells Township. The only wharf in the vicinity at the time belonged to Fort Wayne. Sandwich Township, a Canadian community, lies directly across the Detroit River from Fort Wayne. A hotbed of abolitionist activity, Sandwich Township was heavily populated with former slaves.

Fort Wayne now belongs to the City of Detroit. The Historic Fort Wayne Coalition was formed by preservation-minded people to help restore the fort and offer quality programming.

Visit www.historicfortwaynecoalition.com to learn more about this organization.

BELLE ISLE | STATUE OF GENERAL ALPHEUS STARKEY WILLIAMS

Central and Inselruhe Avenues

General Alpheus Starkey Williams is Michigan's "citizen general" and considered by many to be the Union's unsung hero. Williams served as commander during numerous important battles and was responsible for several successful assaults and defensive campaigns, yet he never received the recognition for his achievements and service that was bestowed upon others.

Considered one of the best generals to come from our state, many cite the general's lack of connections and West Point pedigree as the reasons he never received the accolades he so deserved.

Born in Connecticut, Williams moved to Detroit at the age of 26 and served the community as a lawyer, judge, postmaster, alderman, bank president, and newspaper publisher and editor. In 1844, he ran unsuccessfully for mayor of Detroit.

When the Civil War broke out, Williams trained the state's first volunteers. Soon after the South Carolina militia attacked Fort Sumter in spring 1861, Governor Austin Blair appointed Williams Brigadier General of Volunteers in the Union Army. In October, 1861, he was called into service to lead Michigan troops with the Army of the Potomac.

Williams and his men saw battle at Cedar Mountain, Antietam, Chancellorsville, Second Winchester, and Gettysburg. Williams had served the Army of the Potomac as brigade commander, division commander and corps commander. In 1863, he was transferred to the Army of the Cumberland and served as commander of the 1st Division of the 20th Corps. During the Atlanta Campaign, Williams fought in the battles at Resaca, New Hope Church, Kolb's Farm, Peach Tree Creek, and the siege and capture of Atlanta. Williams was made commander of the 20th Corps, the first troops to enter Savannah, in November of 1864. The following January, Williams was brevetted the rank of major general. During the Carolina Campaign, Williams saw battle at Averasboro and Bentonville.

Most statues of generals display triumphant leadership. This statue of General Williams, completed in 1921, portrays him as sad. Perhaps sculptor Henry Merwin Shrady, who also designed the Ulysses S. Grant memorial in Washington, D.C., wanted to convey the difficulties Union leaders and soldiers faced during the early years of the war. Or, he wanted to represent Williams' disappointment for never receiving the public recognition he deserved.

Williams sits astride **Plug Ugly**, one of two horses he used during the Civil War and his preferred choice for more grueling duty. Williams survived the brutal war uninjured in large part due to Plug Ugly, who was wounded numerous times. At the Battle of Chancellorsville, a Confederate shell landed under Plug Ugly and exploded, sending both Williams and the horse in the air. Miraculously, Williams was uninjured, and Plug Ugly sustained only mild injuries. Plug Ugly accompanied Williams to Gettysburg. He was retired the following year and died shortly thereafter.

Little attention was paid to this deserving general who fought bravely for over three years to preserve our nation and end slavery. In 1959, his important story was finally told in the book, *From the Canon's Mouth: The Civil War Letters of General Alpheus S. Williams*, published by Wayne State University Press and the Detroit Historical Society. General Williams is buried in Elmwood Cemetery.

BELLE ISLE | CIVIL WAR SOLDIER MONUMENT AND ORLANDO POE MARKER
Central and Muse Roads

A Civil War Soldier Monument, dedicated to the Grand Army of the Republic, can be found here. Nearby, on Picnic Way, is a marker dedicated to **General Orlando M. Poe** Post No. 433.

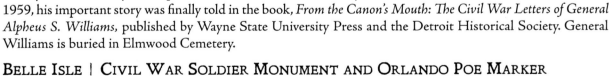

HISTORIC ELMWOOD CEMETERY HISTORY | CONFEDERATE TIES · People buried in Elmwood Cemetery with ties to the Confederacy: Brevet Major General Philip St. George Cooke, father-in-law of legendary Confederate Cavalry Leader Jeb Stuart, remained loyal to the United States and served in the Union Army. Winifred Lee Brent Lyster, author of our state song "**Michigan My Michigan**" was Robert E. Lee's second cousin. Emma Read Berry served as an aide to President Jefferson Davis and assistant secretary of the treasury of the Confederacy.

ELMWOOD CEMETERY

1200 Elmwood Ave. | *(313) 567-3453*

Over 600 men who served the Union during the Civil War are buried at Elmwood Cemetery including 28 generals, three Congressional Medal of Honor recipients, 17 members of the 102nd U.S. Colored Infantry, and **Colonel Thornton Fleming Brodhead**, to whom this guide is dedicated.

The city's oldest cemetery is also the final resting place for many anti-slavery activists such as **George DeBaptiste, William Lambert** and **Dr. Joseph Ferguson** as well as prominent politicians such as Senators **Jacob Merritt Howard** and **Zachariah Chandler**. Some historians claim Senator Chandler's infamous "Blood Letter" which was sent to Governor Austin Blair and released nationally was the real start of the Civil War.

One of the founders of the Republican Party, **Jacob Merritt Howard**, served Detroit and Michigan as city attorney, state representative, and attorney general. A United States senator representing Michigan from 1862 to 1871, Howard fervently voiced his opposition toward the South and believed the Union needed to win the war and reunite the nation. He pressed for the war's conclusion and was active in reconstruction efforts. Howard played a major role drafting the 13th, 14th and 15th Amendments to the U.S. Constitution. The 13th Amendment officially abolished slavery, while the 14th and 15th Amendments granted citizenship to former slaves as well as free blacks and protected their rights as citizens of this country.

A biography distributed by Elmwood Cemetery states:

"Howard left permanent imprints of his work in the Laws of the United States. Few men, other than the founding fathers of our country, have had the opportunity to make their beliefs felt on important Amendments to the Federal Constitution."

The 13th Amendment is inscribed on his gravestone.

Another founder of the Republican Party, **Zachariah Chandler**, was a dry goods merchant whose shrewd investments made him one of the wealthiest men in the state. Chandler served a one-year term as Detroit mayor, four terms as a United States Senator representing Michigan, and later, Secretary of the Interior under President Ulysses S. Grant.

A lifelong opponent to human bondage, Chandler generously provided not only financial support to abolitionist activities, including the Underground Railroad, but muscle as well.

Chandler, once a member of the Whig party, along with other well-built local men who shared the same political philosophy, often appeared en masse on election days to discourage voter intimidation by the city's ruffian element, "which was Democratic in its sympathies."

The Senator was labeled "radical" for his strident opposition to slavery and vocal denunciation of the 1857 Dred Scott Supreme Court decision that upheld the Fugitive Slave Law. He did not support compromise with the South and openly criticized President Lincoln for not taking stronger action immediately against those states that attempted to secede. Chandler sent a strong letter to Governor Austin Blair in which he accused the government of doing nothing. He cited how Generals Washington and Jackson quickly quelled rebellions, yet when six states seceded, the government did nothing but attempt to talk.

The letter, which circulated nationally, stated: "Without a little blood-letting this Union will not, in my estimate, be worth a rush."

Chandler and a group of senators witnessed the disastrous Union defeat at the First Battle of Bull Run. He quickly criticized General George McDowell for not aggressively pursuing victory on the battlefield. After the war, Chandler called Lincoln's plan for Reconstruction "soft". Chandler was a driving force behind the campaign to impeach Lincoln's successor, President Andrew Johnson, whom he viewed as "an incompetent willing to sacrifice all the gains made during the war."

A massive headstone and an impressive mausoleum, in remembrance of two Civil War soldiers **Joseph S. Keen** and **Russell A. Alger** respectively, flank the main road at the cemetery entrance.

The English-born Keen was awarded the Congressional Medal of Honor for carrying and reporting information on enemy troop movements near the Chattahoochee River. A member of the 13th Michigan Infantry, Keen was wounded and captured in 1863 at Chickamauga, Georgia. He was confined to three Confederate prisons at Richmond, Danville and Andersonville before escaping. As he fled, Keen observed the movement of General Hood's forces crossing the Chattahoochee River in an attempt to flank General Sherman's army in the rear. A daring Keen made his way through Confederate encampments on his way to Union lines where he reported this vital information.

Born in Ohio, General Russell A. Alger played a prominent role in Michigan history. In 1884, he was elected as the 20th governor of Michigan and later served the state as a United States senator. During President McKinley's administration, General Alger was appointed Secretary of War.

Alger enlisted in the 2nd Michigan Cavalry at the outbreak of the Civil War and was appointed Captain of Company C. His later commissions included: Major in the 2nd Michigan Cavalry, Lieutenant Colonel in the 6th Michigan Cavalry and Colonel in the 5th Michigan Cavalry.

Wounded four times during the war, Alger participated in over 60 battles and skirmishes including Booneville, Mississippi; Gettysburg, Pennsylvania and the 1964 Shenandoah Valley Campaign, Virginia. At the Battle of Booneville on July 11, 1862, Alger was wounded and captured by the enemy but managed to escape the same day. At the war's end, he was brevetted to the rank of brigadier general followed by major general. In 1889, General Alger was elected commander-in-chief of the Grand Army of the Republic. In this role, he helped improve pensions for Civil War veterans.

Lewis Cass, one of Michigan's most influential political figures is buried at Elmwood Cemetery. He served as the second Territorial Governor and as a U.S. senator representing Michigan. In 1848, Cass lost a bid for president. Appointed Secretary of State under President James Buchanan, he resigned from this position amidst frustation over the president's failure to protect federal interests in the South and lack of federal military action that may have prevented secession.

DETROIT'S FIRST MEMORIAL DAY CELEBRATION · History books state Memorial Day, originally designated as Decoration Day, was first celebrated in Detroit in 1869. Detroit's first observance of the holiday actually occurred one year earlier on May 30th at Elmwood Cemetery.

Quickly organized on three days' notice, the ceremony took place opposite the cemetery entrance with national flags and a stuffed eagle forming the background to the speakers and the Fort Wayne Band.

Thomas R. Williams, who attained rank of brigadier general of U.S. Volunteers, is buried in the family plot. He is the son of John R. Williams, a prominent military figure and Detroit's first mayor who served the city in this capacity for five terms.

The younger Williams' lengthy military career ended when he was shot in the chest at the Battle of Baton Rouge where he and troops under his command defended Louisiana's capital city from Confederate recapture.

Numerous references are made about Thomas Williams in *A Confederate Girl's Diary*, a popular memoir written by Sarah Morgan Dawson.

Of special interest is the grave of **Brevet Major General Philip St. George Cooke**. Cooke serves as a reminder of how the Civil War divided not only the nation but families as well. This Virginian and career military man was the father of Confederate Brigadier General John Rogers Cooke, father-in-law of Confederate Cavalry Leader Jeb Stuart and uncle of author John Esten Cooke, who also served in the Confederate army. General Cooke chose to stay and serve the Union rather than fight with the Confederacy.

"I owe Virginia little, my country much, I shall remain under her flag as it waves the sign of National Constitution Government." said Cooke.

Elmwood Cemetery features a Civil War Memorial lot purchased by the State of Michigan in 1874 to be used exclusively for the internment of deceased Michigan soldiers and sailors who served in this war. This section contains the remains of 205 officers and men who fought in the Civil War, and is one of the few places where the flag is flown both day and night in tribute to those patriots.

The names of those buried at Elmwood Cemetery with ties to the Civil War are too numerous to list here. You'll find **Brigadier General Cyrus O. Loomis**, of the famed Loomis Battery A of the Michigan Light Artillary; **Frank Robinson**, the drummer boy for the 102nd United States Colored Troops (1st Michigan Colored Infantry); **Julian Dickenson**, Captain of the 4th Michigan Cavalry, the regiment responsible for capturing Confederate President Jefferson Davis; **Jane Tinsdale**, Civil War nurse; and **Winifred Lee Brent Lyster**, author of our state song "Michigan, My Michigan." Mrs. Lyster was also the second cousin of Robert E. Lee.

All the stories of these deserving people need to be told, so take the time to fully explore this historic cemetery. Books and maps are available for sale at the cemetery office including *Elmwood Endures: History of a Detroit Cemetery* by Michael S. Franck.

CAMP BACKUS

Opposite Elmwood Cemetery Entrance

Built in 1862, Camp Backus was a new cantonment used for recruiting, replacement and discharge. Originally barracks for 10,000 men were erected. Shortly after the war, the fort was torn down. Nothing exists today to indicate a fort stood there.

CAMP WARD | 1ST MICHIGAN COLORED REGIMENT MARKER

Ralph J. Bunche Elementary/Middle School | *2715 Macomb Street*

Initially, the United States government rejected offers by black men to fight on behalf of the Union. During the second year of war, opinion changed when the army needed more manpower.

When President Lincoln issued the Emancipation Proclamation (September 1862), an executive order freeing all slaves in the Confederate States of America that did not return to Union control by a specified date, the door opened allowing black men to serve in the army.

Many northern states moved quickly to organize black troops, and many Michigan men left to join these regiments.

Henry Barns, editor of *The Detroit Advertiser and Tribune*, petitioned to organize a regiment in Michigan. Barns became colonel of the 1st Michigan Colored Infantry in August of 1862, after Governor Austin Blair received permission to organize a black regiment.

On February 23, 1963, the 1st Michigan Colored Infantry organized at Camp Ward, a farm located where Bunche Elementary/Middle School now stands. Eight hundred and forty-five men from Detroit, southern Michigan and Ontario, Canada volunteered for the regiment. Some were escaped slaves, some fought to free family members still enslaved and others fought to ensure the rights enjoyed by Americans were granted to all.

Black soldiers served under white officers and received less pay than their white counterparts. They also endured inferior conditions. A report claimed the Camp Ward barracks were unfit for human habitation and stated better conditions could be found in any Detroit barn or pig-sty.

Freed slave **Sojourner Truth** resided in Battle Creek and traveled throughout Michigan and other northern states speaking out against slavery and promoting equal rights for women. In 1863, she organized a food drive in Battle Creek for the soldiers stationed at Camp Ward.

When the state of Michigan transferred control of the regiment to the federal government, the 1st Michigan became part of the 102nd U.S. Colored Infantry. A state historic marker commemorating the 1st Michigan Colored Infantry can be found at this site.

DETROIT BARRACKS | 17TH MICHIGAN VOLUNTEER INFANTRY TRAINING SITE

1395 Antietam | (Gratiot and Russell area)

A bronze tablet identifying this site as the Detroit Barracks once hung on the outside wall of the Leland School that once stood here. The marker was placed there in 1925 by Daughters of the Grand Army of the Republic.

The Detroit Barracks, commanded by **Lieutenant Ulysses S. Grant** from 1849 to 1851, served as a training ground during the Civil War. In 1862, the 17th Michigan Volunteer Infantry mustered here under the command of **Colonel William H. Withington**. Made up primarily of men from south-central Michigan, the regiment consisted of "raw recruits from field, workshop and schoolroom." One company was made up almost entirely by students from Ypsilanti Normal School now known as Eastern Michigan University.

The 17th Michigan Volunteers were nicknamed the "Stonewall Regiment" for their bravery exhibited at South Mountain during the Maryland Campaign just a few short weeks after leaving Detroit. The fighting began early on September 14, 1862, and the 17th held its position for hours. At 4 p.m., the command was given for an assault along the entire Union line. The Confederates came out of the woods to meet the charge at a fence line in the middle of the field. Then they moved back to the stone walls along the crest of the hill. The 17th advanced and captured the stone walls.

More Medals of Honors (8) were awarded to members of the 17th Michigan Infantry than any other Michigan regiment. Company B, 47th Ohio, composed of Michigan men, also earned eight medals.

CAMPUS MARTIUS PARK

Woodward and Michigan Avenue

Campus Martius, a popular urban park and gathering space, is the site of the state's foremost Civil War memorial, the Soldiers and Sailors Monument. Designed by American sculptor Randolph Rogers, it's one of Detroit's oldest pieces of public art and one of the first national monuments to honor Civil War veterans.

In 1865, former **Governor Austin Blair** established an association to collect funds so that a monument dedicated to Michigan soldiers and sailors killed during the Civil War could be erected. Detroit, the state's largest city, won the right to display this tribute.

Made of granite and bronze, and standing over 60 feet tall, the classical revival monument features medallion portraits of President Lincoln, Generals Grant and Sherman and Admiral Farragut along with four male statues which depict the four branches of the United States Army: Infantry, Cavalry, Artillery and Navy.

Four female, figures resting on pedestals above the male figures represent Victory, Union, Emancipation and History. While no proof exists to support this belief, local lore suggests renowned African-American abolitionist and women's rights advocate Sojourner Truth served as Roger's inspiration behind the statue Emancipation.

A female figure, personifying a victorious Michigan, crowns the monument. Wearing a winged helmet and brandishing a sword and shield, the 3,800 pound statue depicts Michigan as strong, proud and brave. The inscription below reads:

"Erected by the people of Michigan in honor of the martyrs who fell and the heroes who fought in defence of liberty and union."

The monument was unveiled in April 1872 at a ceremony attended by throngs of people. In fact, the city could barely accommodate all who turned out. Civil War generals in attendance included George Armstrong Custer, Ambrose Burnside, Philip Sheridan, Thomas J. Wood and John Cook.

The 1st Michigan Infantry, the first western regiment to arrive in Washington, D.C., received its colors in a ceremony at Campus Martius. Nearly all the citizens of Detroit turned out to attend this ceremony. Following President Lincoln's assassination, a memorial mass meeting was held here and consisted of the largest assemblage of people in Detroit up to that time.

A two-sided plaque dedicated to the **24th Michigan Infantry and Iron Brigade** can be found at Campus Martius. The 24th Michigan is known as the regiment "born of a riot."

In July 1862, recruiting efforts were underway at Campus Martius to raise a new regiment called the 23rd Michigan. Recruiting events were huge social affairs designed to invoke patriotism and get men to sign up on the spot. These events included guest speakers, military bands and decorations.

Confederate supporters brought in from Canada were planted in the crowd and sparked dissent. Others mistakenly believed a draft was being imposed and began protesting. The celebration quickly turned into a riot.

The embarrassing incident tarnished not only the recruiting effort, but questioned the patriotism of Detroit, Wayne County and even Michigan. Within a few days and without incident, a new regiment, the 24th Michigan Infantry, was raised.

The 24th Michigan, part of the famed Iron Brigade, opened the Battle of Gettysburg on July 1, 1863, and was almost destroyed while holding off Confederate advances until Union forces could get into position. They suffered the highest casualty (80%) rate of any regiment in the battle. This regiment was called upon to escort the funeral procession of slain President Lincoln. U.S. 12/Michigan Avenue, extending from Woodward and across the state, is named the Iron Brigade Memorial Highway in tribute to their service.

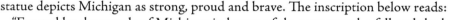
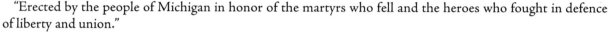

CONFEDERATE SYMPATHIZER AND LEGENDARY LADY OUTLAW BECOMES DETROIT JAILBIRD · During the Civil War, teenager Belle Shirley reported the positions of Union troops to the Confederacy. Her brother Bud and childhood friend Cole Younger along with Frank and Jesse James fought for the Confederacy as part of William C. Quantrill's guerillas.

Later, Belle Shirley became the legendary lady outlaw Belle Starr who served a brief prison stint in the Detroit House of Correction.

RACE RIOT OF 1863

Monroe and Beaubien Streets between Lafayette and Congress

"The bloodiest day that ever dawned upon Detroit" is how a local newspaper described the events of March 6, 1863, as a mob of angry white men swept through the streets of this predominantly black section of town and set homes and businesses on fire and stoned and beat the residents. One man died as a result of the riot. An account describes how an infant was thrown to the ground and almost beaten to death after being wretched from its mother's arms. Fearing for their lives, many African American residents fled to Canada.

City officials responded slowly to the crisis. Order wasn't restored until late evening after Federal troops from nearby Fort Wayne and Ypsilanti finally arrived. By then, serious damage from fire, looting and vandalism had already occurred.

What caused this riot? A rape accusation of a local tavern keeper, who until the time of the accusation, was believed to be white, ignited deep-rooted prejudices. The previous month, two girls, one white and one black, accused William Faulkner of rape .

Faulkner claimed Spanish-Indian heritage, and public records indicated he was a registered voter. Both local newspapers, however, consistently reported him as "Negro." The nature of the crime, coupled with a white victim and black perpetrator, incensed many in the white community.

When Faulkner's trial began on March 5th, an angry crowd gathered outside the courthouse to await a verdict. They pummeled Faulkner with stones as he was escorted back to jail. The next day, an even larger crowd assembled. Anger permeated the air, and any blacks passing through risked verbal and physical abuse.

Found guilty and sentenced to life in prison, Faulkner was showered with bricks and stones as he and the guards made their way back to jail. Guards tried to quell the angry mob by firing a round of blanks into the crowd. They followed with a round of bullets and killed an innocent bystander.

A white man killed at the expense of a Negro? The crowd went crazy and descended upon a nearby house occupied by a black family, terrorizing them with fire and rocks. The ugly scene quickly escalated and spread throughout the area.

After the riot, the Detroit Advertiser and Tribune, a radical Republican paper, labeled the mob a "Free Press mob." The paper further accused the Democratic leaning Detroit Free Press of inciting the riot by intending to: "Excite the ignorant and prejudiced against the negro primarily, and secondarily against the Republicans."

DETROIT PUBLIC LIBRARY | BURTON HISTORICAL COLLECTION

5201 Woodward Ave., Detroit | (313) 833-1000 | fees may apply to special areas of the library

A Civil War picture album of the 3rd Michigan Cavalry is located within the Detroit Public Library's Burton Historical Collection. It consists of 74 *cartes de visite* photographs of regimental members taken between 1861 and 1864. CDVs or calling cards used from 1860 to 1890 became popular collectables during the Civil War. Digital reproductions of all photographs have been made and are available for viewing.

The library also houses many interesting documents pertinent to this era. The Lincoln Collection features letters, Civil War commission appointments, etc. Of special interest are telegrams sent to Michigan Governor Austin Blair by President Lincoln. One telegram requesting more troops sent July 3, 1862 states: "...the quicker you send the fewer you will have to send - time is everything - please act in view of this."

Another document signed by President Lincoln dated Jan 4, 1865, allows "Miss Cloud to pass Union lines 'with ordinary baggage' to return home to Virginia." And a letter dated October 15, 1860, was sent to Lincoln as he campaigned for president by 11-year old Grace Bedell of Westfield, New York advising him to cover his thin face with whiskers. Grace wrote: "All the ladies like whiskers and they would tease their husbands to vote for you and then you would be President."

The 46 volume set of the *Record of Service of Michigan Volunteers* is available in the library Reading Room. For a fee, visitors can access materials in storage such as the *Roster of Union Soldiers* and *Roster of Confederate Soldiers*.

The Hackley Collection features sheet music published between 1799 and 1922. Song themes cover early 19th century plantation life and the Civil War era. Period songs composed by African American musicians are included in this collection.

HART PLAZA | CONFEDERATES BOARD LOCAL STEAMER

Woodward and Jefferson Avenues

No marker denotes the spot, but the riverfront dock was once located near the foot of Woodward, now Hart Plaza. On September 19, 1864, John Yates Beall, a veteran Confederate blockade runner, and 20 co-conspirators working out of Canada boarded the packet steamer **Philo Parsons** at her dock near the foot of Woodward. They dressed as ordinary citizens as to not rouse suspicion. The Philo Parsons traveled regularly between Detroit and Sandusky making stops along the way in Sandwich and Amherstburg, Ontario, as well as Put-in-Bay and other Lake Erie islands.

At the Canadian stops, more southern agents boarded, again disguised as ordinary passengers. While Canada, known then as British North America, remained neutral and opposed slavery, political sympathies leaned to the South, making it easier for Confederate conspirators to devise and launch attacks against the Union from there.

When the steamer entered Lake Erie, agents produced weapons and seized control of the vessel. Their goal was to capture the U.S.S. Michigan, a warship guarding Lake Erie, and the Union prison located on Johnson's Island. Their plan then was to release thousands of Confederate prisoners held on the island. Federal counterspies learned of the plan and alerted the captain of the U.S.S. Michigan, thereby thwarting this bold attempt to free Confederate prisoners-of-war.

HART PLAZA | LINCOLN BUST

Woodward and Jefferson Avenues

This monument by Gutzon Borglum, sculptor of Mount Rushmore, can be found among the many monuments at Hart Plaza and pays tribute to President Lincoln, the 16th president of the United States. Mr. Borglum created the six ton, marble Lincoln head originally exhibited at the White House during the presidency of Theodore Roosevelt that now stands in the Capitol Rotunda in Washington, D.C. Grandiose displays of heroic nationalism and patriotism sweeping the nation at the time appealed to Mr. Borglum's artistic sensibilities. He was commissioned to create the statue dedicated to General Philip Sheridan that stands prominently in Washington, D.C.'s Sheridan Circle. Other works can be found throughout the United States.

Mr. Borglum was originally commissioned to create a memorial to the heroes of the Confederacy planned for Stone Mountain, Georgia. Claiming the proposed 20-foot image of Robert E. Lee would be dwarfed against the massive mountain, he suggested a high-relief frieze - the size of which had never been attempted before - featuring Lee, Jefferson Davis, and "Stonewall" Jackson riding around the mountain, followed by a legion of artillery troops. During the project, disagreements ensued, and Borglum was abruptly dismissed. Known for his temper, Borglum destroyed the models he created for the project. While all traces of his work were wiped away when a new artist was engaged, the spirit of his original design remains.

HART PLAZA | GATEWAY TO FREEDOM

Jefferson Ave. | downtown Detroit

This international memorial to the Underground Railroad is an impressive work by sculptor Ed Dwight. The bronze and granite sculpture is dedicated to the enslaved people who escaped the shackles of bondage and traversed this secretive and treacherous trail in search of freedom and to those who helped them in their flight. Perched symbolically at the edge of the Detroit River, the Gateway to Freedom represents the final steps to freedom.

Across the river in Windsor, Ontario (Canada) the Tower of Freedom stands representing the end of a long, dangerous struggle for freedom and a new beginning. The Tower of Freedom depicts a Quaker woman greeting two emancipated people.

MARINERS' CHURCH

170 East Jefferson Ave. | *(313) 259-2206*

Organized in 1842 to watch over the spiritual well being of sailors and the greater community, the current stone structure of Mariners' Church was consecrated in 1849. With its proximity to the Detroit River, it wasn't long before the church became a point on the Underground Railway. Basement tunnels led former slaves to the waterfront and on to freedom. In 1955, the church was moved 900 feet east to its current location.

LITTLE ROCK MISSIONARY BAPTIST CHURCH

9000 Woodward Ave. | *at Alger Street*

Gorgeous Gothic-style church built in 1928 and designed by George Mason features a beautiful stained glass window of **President Abraham Lincoln** holding the Emancipation Proclamation. Another window that was part of the initial construction pays tribute to our nation's first president, George Washington. Both windows were designed by A. K. Herbert.

The former Central Woodward Christian Church became Little Rock Missionary Baptist Church in 1978 when the building was sold to the new congregation. The new congregation installed more magnificent stained glassed windows which pay tribute to Dr. Martin Luther King, Jr. representing the social gospel, several promi-

nent preachers, and nine of the new 18' windows depict the Stations of the Cross.

GRAND ARMY OF THE REPUBLIC BUILDING

1942 Grand River Ave.

Designed by architect Julian Hess, the GAR Building is one of the oldest buildings in Detroit.

Construction began in 1887 and was completed in 1890. Originally built for the Detroit members of the Grand Army of the Republic, the building featured 13 shops and a bank on the ground floor, office space on the second and third floors, and a small auditorium on the fourth floor.

On February 13, 1986, the building was added to the National Register of Historic Places. A media production company recently purchased the building to house their company and other business interests. Two of the principles are descendents of Civil War veterans.

CHARLES H. WRIGHT MUSEUM OF AFRICAN AMERICAN HISTORY

315 East Warren Ave. at Brush St. | *(313) 494-5800*

Exhibits tell the story of African American history beginning with prehistoric Africa to ancient and modern cultures that evolved on the continent. The journey continues across the Atlantic Ocean with exhibits depicting the horrors of bondage, the harrowing escape to freedom via the Underground Railroad and the fight for equality and emancipation.

Exhibits pay tribute to famous African Americans such as **Frederick Douglass** and **Sojourner Truth**, who played major roles in the fight for freedom, as well as the efforts of everyday men and women who built families, businesses, educational institutions, spiritual traditions, civic organizations and a legacy of freedom and justice in past and present-day Detroit.

WILLIAM WEBB HOUSE

North Side of Congress near St. Antoine | *house no longer exists*

William Webb was a prominent black leader and abolitionist in Detroit. In 1859, he entertained two leading abolitionists in his home. Many attribute the plan revealed by one of the guests that evening as the real beginning of the Civil War. **Frederick Douglass**, a former slave born to a slave mother and white man, was a renowned author, editor and eloquent speaker who delivered moving speeches on the evils of slavery. He had given one of his stirring lectures prior to his appearance at the Webb House.

John Brown, the outspoken and radical abolitionist who promoted armed insurrection as a means to free slaves, and fifteen escaped slaves – one whom had been born en route – were also in town. After delivering the escaped slaves to conductors of the Underground Railroad for safe transfer to Canada, Brown stopped by the Webb house.

There Brown revealed his plan to seize the federal arsenal at Harpers Ferry. Although Douglass called the plan a grave mistake and warned Brown he'd never get out alive, Brown received promises of support from several guests before moving on to Ontario where he recruited a band of followers.

Next Brown set out for Harpers Ferry with 21 men - four free blacks, one fugitive slave and 16 whites, two of whom were his sons. They captured the federal armory and arsenal and Hall's Rifle Works, a supplier of weapons to the government. The group rounded up sixty prominent citizens and held them hostage, hoping their slaves would rise up and join the fight. No slaves came forth.

Instead, the local militia cornered Brown and his men, killing eight of the 22-man army. Troops under the leadership of U.S. Army Colonel Robert E. Lee were dispatched to quell the uprising.

In the end, ten of Brown's men were killed, seven captured and five escaped. An injured Brown and the other captives were taken to Charlestown, Virginia (now Charles Town, West Virginia) where they were quickly tried, sentenced and executed.

The statements made by John Brown during the trial reached the nation. His righteous indignation toward slavery inspired many and swayed public opinion. Therefore, it is been said that the raid ultimately hastened the advent of the Civil War. A historic marker stands at 633 E. Congress to identify the site where Frederick Douglass and John Brown met.

FINNEY HOUSE BARN

Northeast corner of State and Griswold

Abolitionist **Seymour Finney** was a tailor by trade but later opened a hotel called Temperance House. It was in this role as innkeeper that Finney aided numerous fugitive slaves seeking refuge on their way to Canada from 1833 through the Civil War. Detroit played an important role in the Underground Railroad as it was the last stop before Canada. If a fugitive slave reached Detroit, he or she was considered relatively safe.

Finney's Temperance House was located at the southeast corner of Wood-

ward and Gratiot where Kern's Department store once stood in later years. The Kern's clock marks the spot. The hotel's stable where fugitive slaves hid was located a block away at the northeast corner of State and Griswold, across the street from the site of Michigan's first state capitol.

A plaque presented to the city of Detroit in 1926 marks the location of the former stable and station on the Underground Railroad. The plaque proclaims the Detroit Anti-Slavery Society organized in 1837 liberated thousands of slaves. A historic marker can also be found across the street in Capitol Park. Seymour Finney is buried in Woodmere Cemetery.

UNDERGROUND RAILROAD STATION AND BOOKSTORE

Second Baptist Church | 441-461 Monroe Street | (313) 961-0325

Visit the Second Baptist Church's *Connection to Freedom* and take a historical ride aboard a train that traveled without tracks. Sit in the Crogan Street Station and hear the story of oppressed people escaping slavery who rested in secret at Second Baptist Church before crossing the Detroit River to Canada on the T. Whitney, a boat belonging to church member **George DeBaptiste**.

"Thirteen former enslaved Christians" founded the church in 1836 that housed the important Crogan Street Station, a vital link in the complex and secret national network of Underground Railroad stations. Crogan Street later became Monroe.

GEORGE DEBAPTISTE HOME

Southwest corner of East Larned and Beaubien | home no longer exists

A famous Michigan stockholder, black businessman, and member of the Second Baptist Church of Detroit, **George DeBaptiste** claimed to have personally assisted 108 fugitive slaves escape to freedom before coming to Michigan in 1846. His trading business enabled him to travel via steamboat between cities, giving him the perfect opportunity to hide fugitive slaves aboard. DeBaptiste also worked as a personal valet to General William Henry Harrison during his presidential campaign and then accompanied him to the White House as a steward.

In Detroit, DeBaptiste was active in Underground Railroad and antislavery activities. He served as a delegate to the Cleveland National Convention of Colored Citizens and as an agent for the Freedman's Aid Commission. During the Civil War, he helped organize the 1st Michigan Colored Regiment. A historical marker identifies the spot where DeBaptiste's house once stood.

WILLIAM LAMBERT HOME

Northeast corner of East Larned and St. Aubin | home no longer exists

William Lambert, a tailor by trade and successful businessman, served as the manager and treasurer of the Detroit Terminal of the Underground Railroad and headed the Detroit Vigilance Committee.

Considered to be the city's leading black abolitionist at the time, Lambert was present at the 1859 meeting between **John Brown** and **Frederick Douglass** at William Webb's house. Lambert even made a financial contribution toward Brown's plan of raiding Harpers Ferry. Lambert organized the first State Convention of Colored Citizens and urged blacks to participate directly in their struggle for freedom and equality.

A historic marker identifies the site of William Lambert's home.

HISTORIC FIRST CONGREGATIONAL CHURCH OF DETROIT

33 E. Forest Ave. | (313) 831-4080

Established in 1844, the first two churches were located at Fort and Wayne Streets. The basement of the second church hid refugees of the Underground Railroad as they awaited passage across the Detroit River to freedom

in Canada. The current church, a magnificent example of Victorian architecture, offers the *Living Museum's Underground Railroad Flight to Freedom*, an experiential tour that draws upon storytelling and simulation (participant wrists are shackled) to recreate the harsh journey enslaved people faced on their way to freedom. Public and private tours available daily. Contact church for full details.

GRAND CIRCUS PARK

Woodward Ave. and East Adams

In this half-circle shaped park flanking both sides of Woodward, you'll find several interesting statues. One prominent statue immortalizes **Hazen S. Pingree**, a four-term mayor of Detroit and Michigan's 24th governor. Seated in a chair above the words "Idol of the People," this revered citizen was a veteran of the Civil War who served in the 1st Massachusetts Heavy Artillery where he was captured and confined to several different Confederate prisons including Andersonville.

During General Sherman's "March to the Sea", Pingree was transferred to a prison in Millen, Georgia where he escaped during roll call after pretending to be someone else. Pingree was witness to General Lee's surrender at Appomattox Court House in Virginia on April 9, 1865.

The fountain at Grand Circus Park pays tribute to **General Russell A. Alger** *(see Elmwood Cemetery entry)*.

GENERAL GRANT HOUSE

Eight Mile and Woodward | Michigan State Fair Grounds

General Grant's first of two Detroit homes is located here. He resided in Detroit from 1849-1851 when as a lieutenant he commanded the Detroit Barracks. The home was originally located at 253 East Fort Street between Russell and Rivard. The home is now boarded up and its fate unknown. Grant's second home was located on the north east corner of Jefferson and Rivard. A motel occupies the site today.

SKILLMAN BRANCH OF THE DETROIT PUBLIC LIBRARY

Library and Farmer Streets

A statue of **Abraham Lincoln** holding a copy of the 13th Amendment is located here. The base of this reproduction of the Alfonso Pelzer statue once located on the vast grounds of the Lincoln Plant at Warren and Livernois, proclaims "Let Men be Free."

OTHER SITES OF INTEREST IN DETROIT

+ Woodward and Canfield, Detroit, site of the old fairgrounds where the 24th Michigan trained.
+ Detroit Historical Museum located at 5401 Woodward Avenue features an exhibit identifying local stops on the Underground Railroad.
+ Harper Hospital, now part of the Detroit Medical Center, first stood at Woodward and Martin Place. The hospital opened in 1864 to care for those wounded in the Civil War.
+ Captain George Gordon Meade, victor at Gettysburg, resided in Detroit from 1857 to 1861, while he oversaw the Corp of Engineers Great Lakes topographical survey. He resided at 3 Aspinall Terrace which was located at the corner of Bagley and Clifford. The building no longer exists.

Dexter

FOREST LAWN CEMETERY

8000 Grand Street

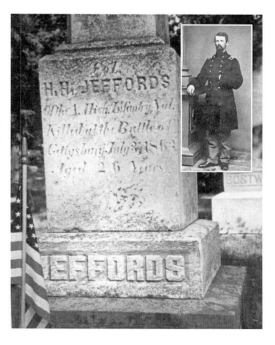

Grave of **Colonel Harrison H. Jeffords** commander of the 4th Michigan Volunteer Infantry can be found here. Jeffords was mortally wounded in the Wheatfield on July 2, 1863, during the second day of the Battle of Gettysburg as he tried to retrieve the regiment's flag which he vowed to protect. Colonel Jeffords was the highest ranking officer to die by bayonet.

MONUMENT PARK

Baker Road at Main Street | downtown

A statue of a Civil War soldier at parade rest stands guard in this park situated in the center of downtown Dexter.

DEXTER AREA HISTORICAL MUSEUM

3443 Inverness Street | (734) 426-2519
Civil War artifacts displayed.

GORDON HALL
8341 Island Lake Road | (734) 426-2519

A historic landmark, this Greek and Antebellum-style home was built in the early 1840s for village founder **Samuel W. Dexter**. The home may have been used as a stop on the Underground Railroad.

VFW POST 557
8225 Dexter-Chelsea Road

Adjacent to the VFW stands the Parrott cannon originally presented to the Harrison Jeffords GAR Post #330.

Dundee
TRIANGLE PARK
Downtown

In the heart of the Village of Dundee's historic triangle district is Triangle Park, home to a beautiful, eight-sided limestone bandstand erected in 1913 as a soldiers' memorial, commemorating service by Dundee boys in the Civil and Spanish American Wars. The Civil War memorial honors the 3rd Michigan Cavalry and the 7th, 15th, 17th and 18th Michigan Infantries. Prominently displayed near the bandstand is a 100 pound Parrot Rifled Siege Cannon.

OLD MILL MUSEUM
242 Toledo St. | (734) 529-8596

This unique museum features three floors of exhibits pertaining to local history including some GAR artifacts.

East Lansing
ALUMNI MEMORIAL CHAPEL
Michigan State University

This Odell Prather stained glass window shows **President Lincoln** signing the Morrill Act of 1862, a bill that provided land to each state to establish colleges that would teach agriculture, science, mechanical science and liberal arts.

Grosse Ile
JAMES VERNOR HOME
7540 Horsemill Rd. | private residence

The **James Vernor** family resided in Detroit for many years, but the Horsemill Road residence was the Civil War veteran's final home. A widower for 36 years, Vernor died at the age of 84 in the upstairs library of this home on October 29, 1927.

Additional information on the prominent Detroit businessman, founder of Vernors Ginger Ale and member of the 4th Michigan Cavalry can be found under the Woodmere Cemetery listing.

COLONEL BRODHEAD'S OFFICE
20604 East River Rd. | private residence

Colonel Thornton Fleming Brodhead served the state of Michigan in many capacities including lawyer, prosecuting attorney, deputy secretary of state and state senator. He was the owner and editor of the *Democratic Free Press* (forerunner to the *Detroit Free Press*) and *Detroit Commercial Bulletin*.

In fact, Brodhead was the first Michigan newspaper publisher to own a steam printing press. In 1853, Brodhead became Detroit Postmaster appointed by President Franklin Pierce.

Brodhead served with distinction during the U.S - Mexican War, earning the rank of full Captain. When the Civil War broke out, he was commissioned to raise a cavalry regiment and became Colonel of the 1st Michigan Cavalry. Mortally wounded at the Second Battle of Bull Run on August 30, 1862, this husband and father of six children was shot point blank by Adjutant Lewis Harman of the 12th Virginia, near Lewis Ford after he refused to surrender. Harman rode off with Brodhead's horse and weapons.

Before dying, Colonel Brodhead penned a letter to his wife stating "General Pope has been outwitted and that McDowell is a traitor. Had they done their duty, as I did mine; and had [they], as I had, the dear old Flag would have waived in triumph. Our Generals—not the Enemy's have defeated us." He ended the letter with a poignant farewell (see guidebook dedication for an excerpt).

Three days before he died, Colonel Brodhead received the deathbed brevet of Brigadier General of the United States Volunteers. He died on September 2, 1862. A historic marker designates the site of his former office. The exterior shell of the building still stands; however, the office is on private property.

GRAY GABLES | THE MAJOR HORACE GRAY HOME

24140 East River Rd. | *private residence*

A prominent businessman, ship-builder, politician, Detroit sheriff, Federal Indian Agent, Civil War officer and early real estate broker, **Major Horace Gray** was an energetic, patriotic, and visionary individual remembered for his love of family, friendship, intelligence, quick wit and public service.

In 1861, Gray returned from the Dakotas where he had served as a Federal Indian Agent for the Sioux Nation at Yankton. At this critical time, many Michigan men were called into active service. Gray was offered a colonelcy but declined. A year later, Major Gray changed his mind and entered the fray. He organized the 4th Michigan Cavalry and in this capacity, became a member of the elite Minty's Sabre Brigade. Major Gray distinguished himself at Chattanooga, where he commanded the Union field force of 600, as well as Chickamauga and Lookout Mountain.

Near the end of the war, Major Gray became ill and returned home to Grosse Ile where he led the life of a gentleman farmer and entrepreneur. Gray's military and tribal expertise was called upon again in 1879 when an entourage that included the President and Mrs. Rutherford B. Hayes and General William Tecumseh Sherman visited him. The party arrived by boat and docked at the foot of Gray Gables.

Horace Gray lived at his Grosse Ile home for fifty years and died there in 1895. He is buried at Detroit's historic Elmwood Cemetery, which he had originally had a hand in creating.

MAJOR GENERAL ORLANDO B. WILLCOX who is buried in Arlington National Cemetery, was from Detroit where he practiced law prior to the Civil War. A West Point graduate, General Willcox commanded the 1st Michigan Infantry, the first Western regiment to arrive in Washington, D.C. following President Lincoln's plea for troops. Captured during the First Battle of Bull Run, General Willcox was sent to a Confederate prison and later released during a prisoner exchange. He received the Medal of Honor for his actions at the First Bull Run. General Willcox remained in the army, advancing to brigade, division and corps commander.

KIRKLAND C. BARKER HOUSE

24808 East River Rd. | private residence

Mayor of Detroit during the final year of the Civil War, **Kirkland C. (K.C.) Barker** became aware of the Confederate plot to hijack the Philo Parson's and capture the U.S.S. Michigan. The Mayor's actions helped thwart what potentially could have been a disastrous situation for the Union.

(See entry under Detroit heading: Confederates Board Local Steamer for more details)

Barker, who established Detroit's first nighttime police force, also thwarted a plan to interrupt the national election of 1864.

Southern sympathizers from Canada hatched a plan to set Canadian border cities such as Detroit afire. They hoped the confusion created by the fires would influence the election's outcome in favor of the South. Barker caught wind of the plan and put it down before anything materialized.

After the war, a friendship developed between Mayor Barker and General Custer, now a Civil War hero. Both George and his wife Elizabeth (Libbie) spent time on Grosse Ile visiting the Barkers. Libbie stayed with the Barkers for weeks at a time during her husband's deployment to Kansas in 1868 and 1869. In her writings, Libbie made reference to the beautiful copper bathtub found in the Barker home where she bathed during her visits.

General Custer himself spent time on Grosse Ile after his court martial and forced one-year removal from duty in 1868. Custer was at the Barker home when he received the telegram from William T. Sherman, calling him back to duty in Kansas, two months before his one-year sentence was up.

An avid yachtsman, Barker and three others, including the 14-year old son of his gardener, drowned in the Detroit River, not far from Barker's Grosse Ile waterfront home.

Aboard the boat Mattie, the four headed out to Stoney Island to retrieve Barker's racing yacht Cora in preparation for the International Boat Club Regatta. The Mattie capsized; all were thrown overboard and drowned. Although his body was not recovered, a tombstone in remembrance of Mayor Barker stands at Elmwood Cemetery.

Hillsdale

Hillsdale was home to **Major General Charles C. Doolittle**, who is buried at Toledo, Ohio's historic Woodlawn Cemetery, and **Colonel George W. Lombard** of the 4th Michigan Infantry. Colonel Lombard died from wounds received in the Battle of the Wilderness, in Virginia on May 6, 1864. The colonel's remains may still be buried on the battlefield, as his body was never identified during later attempts to recover the dead and rebury them.

SULTANA MEMORIAL

29 North Howell Street

Located in front of the Hillsdale County Courthouse, this monument pays tribute to Union soldiers, a large number from Hillsdale County, who were killed in what is known as America's greatest maritime disaster. While the conclusion of the Civil War should have been a time of celebration, this fatal disaster was a sad blow for the families of soldiers who had managed to survive the cruelties of war only to perish upon their return trip home.

The steamboat Sultana departed port in New Orleans on April 21, 1865 bound for St. Louis, Missouri. Legally permitted to carry only 376 passengers, an estimated 2,200 to 2,500 passengers, primarily Union soldiers making their long awaited journey home, boarded in Vicksburg, Mississippi. Many had been incarcerated at Confederate prison camps at Cahaba and Andersonville and were injured and/or sick.

Bursting at the seams with passengers packed into berths and no room to move on deck, the overcrowded ship made its way up river, past Memphis, Tennessee, where it exploded in the early hours of April 27th. An estimated 1,800 passengers either drowned or were blown to bits as a result of the explosion. Of the survivors, several hundred died days later from burns or exposure. Bodies were discovered for months downstream following the disaster and many were never recovered.

Inside the courthouse is a small display of Civil War relics.

ABRAHAM LINCOLN AND LORADO TAFT CIVIL WAR STATUES | HILLSDALE COLLEGE
33 East College Street

Erected in June 1895 by the Alpha Kappa Phi Literary Society, this statue of a Civil War soldier by Lorado Taft, a prominent sculptor from Illinois, pays tribute to the members of the society who served in the Civil War.

The inscription reads: "Our Roll of Honor. Alpha Kappa Phi volunteers in the War of the Rebellion. To the memory of our heroic dead who fell in defense of the Union." The inscription is followed by the names of the members who served. The monument stands prominently on campus in the center of Central, Moss and Delp Halls.

A lifesize statue of President Abraham Lincoln was erected here in 2009.

OAK GROVE CEMETERY
West/East Montgomery Street | west of North Hillsdale Road

Two hundred and twenty Civil War veterans are buried at Oak Grove Cemetery including **Brigadier General Christopher John Dickerson**, originally colonel of the 10th Michigan Infantry. General Dickerson was injured and taken prisoner in February 1864 at Buzzard's Roost, Georgia.

A Civil War soldier monument at parade rest dedicated to those who served can be found in the cemetery.

LEWIS EMERY PARK
2020 State Road

Location of Camp Woodbury, the encampment and training site of the 18th Michigan Infantry in early 1862. This location was chosen because of the healthy natural spring water.

Hudson

HUDSON MUSEUM
219 West Main Street | (517) 448-8858

Nice Civil War display and artifacts of interest including four different kepis and a field desk.

MAPLE GROVE CEMETERY
Maple Grove Avenue and Cadmus Road

Two heroic battery captains from the 1st Michigan Light Artillery lie in rest at the Maple Grove Cemetery: the audacious **Captain Samuel DeGoyler** of Battery H was mortally wounded at Vicksburg, Mississippi and **Captain Jabez Daniels** of Battery I, whose guns helped repulse Pickett's Charge on July 3, 1863, during the Battle of Gettysburg.

Jackson

BIRTHPLACE OF THE REPUBLICAN PARTY

Second and West Franklin Streets

A bronze marker at the northwest corners of Second and Franklin denotes the outdoor location "Under the Oaks" where the first state convention was held on July 6, 1854, by those supporting the end of slavery. Jackson is one of four communities claiming to be the birthplace of the Republican Party. Since a slate of candidates was elected at this convention, Jackson is considered by many to be the true birthplace of the party.

MOUNT EVERGREEN CEMETERY

1047 Greenwood Avenue

Mt. Evergreen is the final resting place of **Governor Austin Blair**, Michigan's 13th governor who's best known as "the Civil War Governor." A founder of the Republican Party, Blair vehemently opposed slavery and southern secession. Governor Blair personally raised approximately $100,000 to equip the 1st Michigan Infantry Volunteer Regiment. President Lincoln relied heavily on the support from Governor Blair and the Michigan regiments he sent.

UNDER THE OAKS

On July 6, 1854, a state convention of anti-slavery men was held in Jackson to found a new political party. *Uncle Tom's Cabin* had been published two years earlier, causing increased resentment against slavery, and the Kansas-Nebraska Act of May, 1854, threatened to make slave states out of previously free territories. Since the convention day was hot and the huge crowd could not be accommodated in the hall, the meeting adjourned to an oak grove on "Morgan's Forty" on the outskirts of the town. Here a state-wide slate of candidates was selected, and the Republican party was born. Winning an overwhelming victory in the elections of 1854, the Republican party went on to dominate national politics throughout the nineteenth century.

Other public tributes to Governor Blair include a historic marker in the city of Eaton Rapids designating the site where Governor Blair lived when he first launched his political career as Eaton Rapids clerk and a grand statue in front of the State Capitol in Lansing.

Brigadier General William H. Withington is also buried at Mt. Evergreen. As colonel, he commanded the 17th Michigan Volunteer Infantry, also known as the Stonewall Regiment, for their brave advancement and capture of the stone wall from Confederate troops during the Battle of South Mountain in Maryland on September 14, 1862, and forcing their retreat. Colonel Withington earned a Medal of Honor for his actions as captain of Company B, 1st Michigan Infantry at the First Battle of Bull Run.

Buried here are **Brigadier General Charles Deland** and **Sergeant Frederick Lyon**. Deland was colonel of the 1st Michigan Sharpshooters and wounded in several battles.

Sergeant Lyon of the 1st Vermont Cavalry was awarded the medal for his actions on October 19, 1864, at the Battle of Cedar Creek, Virginia where he captured a Confederate flag, three officers and an anbulance.

The grave of **Captain Christian Rath** of Company I, 17th Michigan Infantry can be found here as well. Captain Rath was the executioner of four of the eight Lincoln conspirators: David E. Herold, George Atzerodt, Lewis Powell, and Mary E. Surratt. David Herold surrendered when discovered hiding in a barn with John Wilkes Booth. Innkeeper Mary Surratt's role as a co-conspirator earned her the unfortunate distinction of being the first female executed by the United States Federal Government.

A member of Major General Hartranft's staff, who was charged with overseeing the conspirators' imprisonment at the Washington D.C. Arsenal Penitentiary, Captain Rath was selected hangman by the federal government. His responsibilities included setting up the gallows and carrying out the process.

Just before 2 p.m. on July 7, 1865, Captain Rath clapped his hands three times and sent the convicted to their fate. The captain, who received a brevet

MICHIGAN'S OLDEST CIVIL WAR REENACTMENT as well as the largest in the state and the Midwest - takes place annually on the last weekend in August at Cascades Park in Jackson.

of lieutenant colonel for his service, was supposedly haunted by his participation in the executions for the rest of his life.

A bronze and granite Civil War Soldiers Monument stands near the cemetery gate. Jackson resident, Laura Evans, entrusted funds to be used to build the monument in remembrance of those who served in the Civil War and dedicated it in honor of her family members. Created by sculptor Frederick C. Hibbard, who studied under Lorado Taft, the three-figure composition may represent Evan's parents and soldier husband or the parents of any young soldier, watching as he valiantly sets off for war, unsure if he'll ever return.

SITE OF FORMER AUSTIN BLAIR HOME

Lansing Avenue and Blackstone Street

A boulder with bronze tablet proclaims: "Upon this site stood the home of Austin Blair, one of the founders of the Republican Party and Michigan's War Governor 1861-1865."

GOVERNOR AUSTIN BLAIR PARK

Greenwood Avenue and South Jackson Street

Site of a state historical marker dedicated to Michigan's Civil War governor.

STATE OF MICHIGAN ROADSIDE PARK

U.S.-127, south of Jackson

A bronze plaque is dedicated to Governor Austin Blair.

DEFENSE OF THE FLAG AT WITHINGTON PARK

Wildwood and West Michigan Avenues

Also known as the Jackson County Soldiers and Sailors Monument, *Defense of the Flag* is a memorial to the men of the First and Seventeenth Michigan Volunteer Infantry regiments. The monument was erected at the expense of their commander General William H. Withington. Unfortunately, General Withington died in the year prior to the monument's dedication.

In *Outdoor Sculpture*, writer Michael W. Panhorst describes the bronze and granite Lorado Taft monument featuring the regimental battle flag as waving in "the breeze above a defiant standard bearer and two of his valiant comrades. One soldier falls and grasps at the chest wound he has just received. The other kneels, peering into the face of the enemy, his rifle at the ready to defend his flag – a symbol more important to many soldiers than life itself."

ELLA SHARPE MUSEUM OF ART AND HISTORY

3225 Fourth Street | (517) 787-2320

Civil War artifacts are displayed including the "Resolution Table" which was used in the 1854 founding of the Republican Party popularly referred to as "Under the Oaks."

GENERAL ROBERT H.G. MINTY HOME

1912 4th Street | private residence

General Robert Horatio George Minty, commander of the famous Minty's Saber Brigade, lived in this Jackson home from 1869 to 1876. The Irish-born General honed his saber skills as an ensign serving five years in the British Army in the West Indies, Honduras, and the west coast of Africa. Upon his retirement from British military service in 1853, Minty came to the United States. He married Grace Ann Abbott of London, Ontario, and they settled in Detroit.

When the Civil War broke out, Minty became major of the 2nd Michigan Cavalry, followed by lieutenant colonel of the 3rd Michigan and then colonel of the 4th Michigan. In 1863, Minty commanded a cavalry brigade that included the 4th Michigan. The brigade became known for its excellent sabre wielding skills, hence it was nicknamed Minty's Sabre Brigade.

The Sabre Brigade captured Shelbyville, Tennessee in June of 1863. Minty commanded the cavalry on the left at Chickamauga and later covered General Thomas's retreat to Chattanooga. Minty's Sabre Brigade saw action at New Madrid, Farmington, and the Atlanta campaign, where Minty led a division in Kilpatrick's raid around that city. Minty is considered to be one of the top cavalry commanders in the western theater. Had he commanded troops in the eastern theater, many believe Minty would have received more recognition for his contributions to the Union. At the end of the war, Colonel Minty received the brevets of brigadier-general and major-general of volunteers for his distinguished service.

General Minty returned to Michigan and settled in Jackson where he raised 10 children. He later moved west and is buried in Ogden, Utah.

CAMP BLAIR STATE HISTORICAL MARKER

Wildwood Avenue between North Thompson and Hibbard Avenues

Camp Blair operated from 1864 to 1866 and served as a rendezvous point for troops to be mustered out of service. It included a hospital, barracks, storehouse and offices.

Jonesville

SUNSET VIEW CEMETERY

Chicago Road/U.S.-12 | Fayetteville Township

Major General Henry Baxter is buried here. Originally, Lieutenant Colonel of the 7th Michigan Infantry, his brigade played a prominent role during the first day of the Battle of Gettysburg. General Baxter was wounded several different times during the war. The grave of **Ebenezer Oliver Grosvenor** can be found here as well. Grosvenor was Lieutenant Governor of Michigan from 1865-67. *(See entry below.)*

A Civil War soldier monument at parade rest stands in Village Park off U.S. 12.

GROSVENOR HOUSE MUSEUM

211 Maumee Street

This is the renovated home of **Ebenezer Oliver Grosvenor** who was elected 17th Lieutenant Governor of Michigan and served during Governor Henry H. Crapo's first term. In 1861, during Governor Blair's administration, Mr. Grosvenor was commissioned colonel on the governor's staff and became president of the military contract board to which he was appointed. Mr. Grosvenor was head of the commission overseeing the construction of the state's Capitol. Elijah E. Meyers, architect of the Capitol, also designed the Grosvenor home.

Women's Hall of Fame Honors Three Civil War Women

Julia Wheelock Freeman

Julia Wheelock Freeman (1833-1900) known as "The Florence Nightingale of Michigan," spent three years in the hospitals of Washington, D.C., nursing wounded and dying soldiers. A teacher in Palo, Michigan when the Civil War broke out in April 1861, Freeman traveled to our nation's capital when she received news her brother, Orville, was wounded. Although Orville died before she arrived, Freeman saw the desperate need for nurses and remained in Washington. A volunteer with the Michigan Soldiers Relief Association, Freeman endured long hours cooking, cleaning, and comforting Michigan's wounded soldiers sent to recover, and often die, in Washington area hospitals. Freeman's detailed journal and her published memoir, *The Boys in White*, provide invaluable insight into period medical practices, burial procedures, and daily life at the hospitals. Her writings also shed light on local and national events of interest including the assassination of President Abraham Lincoln. Ms. Freeman was inducted into the Michigan Women's Hall of Fame in 2002 for her achievement in the categories of military and nursing.

Sarah Emma Edmonds

Twenty year old Canadian-born Sarah Emma Edmonds (1841 - 1898) was residing in Flint when she disguised herself as a male named Franklin Thompson and joined Company F of the 2nd Michigan Volunteer Infantry Regiment in Detroit on May 25, 1861. As Frank Thompson, Edmonds bravely served in the army as a spy, field nurse, mail carrier and soldier. A master of disguise, Edmonds became adept at espionage and infiltrated Confederate lines 11 times dressed as a black slave, dry goods clerk or even a young Confederate boy. In 1863, Edmonds contracted malaria while in Kentucky and requested a furlough which was denied. Fearful her true identity would be discovered if she sought medical attention, Edmonds left her regiment and never returned. Thus, her alias, Franklin Thompson, was charged with desertion. After her recovery, Edmonds ditched her male disguise and worked as a nurse with the United States Christian Commission. In 1864, she published *Nurse and Spy in the Union Army*, in autobiography that sold over 75,000 copies. Edmonds donated the profits from this popular book to soldiers aid groups. Edmonds attended a 2nd Michigan reunion in 1876 where her comrades welcomed her, many of whom had no clue until after the war that Franklin was actually a woman. In fact, regiment members helped Edmonds in her fight to have the charge of desertion removed from her military records and supported her application for a military pension. In 1884, following an eight year battle and an Act of Congress, Franklin Thompson was cleared of desertion charges and Sara Edmonds awarded his pension. Edmonds, the only woman admitted into the Grand Army of the Republic, died in 1898 at her home in La Porte, Texas. In 1901, she was re-buried will full military honors in Houston's Washington Cemetery. Ms. Edmonds was inducted into the Michigan Women's Hall of Fame in 1992 for her achievement in the category of military.

Annie Blair Etheridge

Detroit's Annie Blair Etheridge (1839 - 1913) joined the 2nd Michigan infantry as the regiment's vivandière, or Daughter of the Regiment, whose purpose was to rally the men in battle and provide aid as needed. Affectionately nicknamed "Gentle Annie" by the soldiers she tended, Etheridge eventually served in the 2nd, 3rd, and 5th Michigan infantry regiments and saw some of the hardest fighting during the Civil War, including the battles of Fair Oaks, Second Bull Run, Chancellorsville, Gettysburg and the Wilderness. Etheridge also served as an army nurse on a hospital transport as well as in an army hospital and was awarded the Kearny Cross for the bravery and courage she demonstrated during the Civil War. The medal was named in honor of Major General Philip Kearney, commander of the First Division, Third Army Corps, who was killed at the battle of Chantilly, September 1, 1862. After the war, Etheridge was eventually given a $25 month pension for her unpaid military service. Upon her death in 1913, Etheridge was buried with full military honors in Arlington National Cemetery. Ms. Etheridge was inducted into the Michigan Women's Hall of Fame in 2010 for her achievement in the categories of military and nursing.

Lansing
MICHIGAN HISTORICAL MUSEUM

702 West Kalamazoo Street | *(517) 373-3559*

An entire section of the Michigan Historical Museum is dedicated to a permanent exhibit of Michigan in the Civil War featuring guns, swords and accessories from Michigan soldiers. The unique Henry rifle once belonging

to Battle Creek's **Sergeant Lorenzo Barker** of Company D, 66th Illinois Infantry is displayed. Engraved on the gun's breech are the battles in which Barker fought.

The museum cares for and stores over 150 of Michigan's blood-stained and sacred Civil War battle flags. This precious collection consists of: the original flag of the Michigan Cavalry Brigade, the individual flags of the regiments comprising this esteemed brigade, the tattered 24th Michigan Infantry's national colors from Gettysburg, and flags from other Michigan regiments and batteries.

The flag exhibit can be accessed online at www.seekingmichigan.org.

STATE OF MICHIGAN ARCHIVES

702 West Kalamazoo Street | *(517) 373-1408*

The archives house primary resources from the Civil War including regimental records, letters, diaries, photographs, newspaper articles, book, etc. Many records from this collection have been digitized and can be viewed online at SeekingMichigan.com.

STATE OF MICHIGAN CAPITOL BUILDING

100 N. Capitol Avenue

Reproductions of Michigan's coveted Civil War regimental flags can be viewed on the first floor of the Capitol rotunda. The original 157 tattered, bloody and bullet-ridden flags hung from the rotunda, a proud testament to those from our great state who served and sacrificed in order to preserve the Union. Unfortunately, age and exposure caused the flags to deteriorate, so they were moved to the Michigan Historical Museum for safe storage and repair.

Several notable Civil War monuments can be found on the capital grounds in the area called Capitol Square. A bronze statue of Michigan's Civil War **Governor Austin Blair** is the first and only statue of a person found in the square. Dedicated on October 12, 1898, the statue was designed by Edward Clark Potter who also designed the equestrian monuments of General Custer in Monroe and Generals Sedgwick and Slocum in Gettysburg. Monuments honoring the 1st Michigan Engineers

BUCKSKIN BESTED BOOTH ◂ Buckskin was the horse used by Secret Service agent Luther Byron Baker to track Lincoln assassin John Wilkes Booth to the Virginia barn where the fugitive met his demise. The horse became famous when he joined Baker onstage during lectures where Baker gave his account of the assassin's capture. Photos of Buckskin with the details of the Booth pursuit printed on the backside became coveted souvenirs. When Buckskin died, a taxidermist preserved the horse and he again shared the stage with Baker on the lecture circuit. Buckskin was later donated to the Michigan State University Museum.

and Mechanics and 1st Michigan Sharpshooters are present along with a boulder and bronze tablet erected by the Department of Michigan Women's Relief Corps on June 11, 1924, in memory of the Grand Army of the Republic.

MICHIGAN WOMEN'S HISTORICAL CENTER AND HALL OF FAME
213 W. Malcolm X Street

The center has inducted the following women from this era into the Women's Hall of Fame for their contributions in the area of abolition, military, and/or nursing: **Elizabeth Margaret Chandler, Sara Emma Edmonds, Annie Etheridge, Julia Wheelock Freeman, Laura Smith Haviland, Eliza Seaman Leggett** and **Sojourner Truth.**

MOUNT HOPE CEMETERY
1709 Mount Hope Avenue

Assistant Surgeon George E. Ranney of the 2nd Michigan Cavalry is buried here. Ranney was awarded the Medal of Honor for bravery exhibited during the Battle of Resaca in Georgia on May 14, 1864. Aware he could sustain serious injuries or even be killed, Ranney selflessly put himself in harm's way as he rescued wounded soldiers and carried them to safety.

    First Lieutenant Luther Byron Baker, who assisted the Secret Service in pursuit of President Lincoln's assassinator John Wilkes Booth, is buried here as well. Baker tracked Booth to the Virginia barn that was set afire after Booth refused to surrender. When Booth wouldn't leave the burning barn, he was shot and mortally wounded by Sergeant Boston Corbett of the 16th New York Cavalry.

    The Civil War section of the cemetery contains 50 headstones and Lansing's official Civil War monument. Erected in 1877, the monument was rededicated in October 2007 by descendants of Civil War veterans.

Mason

INGHAM COUNTY COURT HOUSE
341 South Jefferson Street

Recently dedicated Ingham County Civil War Memorial honors its soldiers who died in the Civil War.

MAPLE GROVE CEMETERY
East and Columbia Streets

Lieutenant Colonel Amos E. Steele is buried here. He was killed in battle on July 3, 1865, while valiantly commanding the 7th Michigan Infantry during the repulse of Pickett's Charge at the Battle of Gettysburg.

Milan

MARBLE PARK CEMETERY
520 West Main Street

A nice Civil War soldier monument at parade rest can be found here.

RICE CEMETERY
South of Milan on Dennison Road

Medal of Honor recipient Sergeant Daniel McFall of the 17th Infantry, Company E, is buried here. Sergeant McFall earned his medal for his actions on May 12, 1864 at Spotsylvania where he captured a Confederate colonel leading a brigade and also rescued his lieutenant from enemy capture.

Monroe

MONROE COUNTY HISTORICAL MUSEUM

126 South Macomb St. | *(734) 240-7780*

Prominent regiments, influential politicians and major military figures hailed from Monroe County. The county produced five generals, seven colonels and eight Medal of Honor recipients with **Lieutenant Tom Custer** the first double honoree in our nation's history. Several exhibits illustrate the contributions by residents of this era and include coveted items such as a captain's frock coat belonging to **Norman Hall**, a colonel's frock coat be-

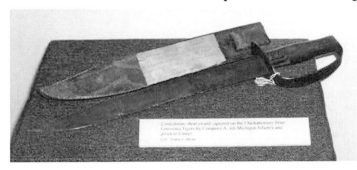

longing to **Brigadier General George Spalding** and the regimental flag of the 7th Michigan Infantry with its hand-embroidered moniker "The Forlorn Hope At Fredericksburg."

Museum archives house correspondence, diaries, records, and photographs from the Civil War kept by Custer family members and the community, an original set of the *Record of Service of Michigan Volunteers in the Civil War*, known as the brown books, which provide detailed information on Michigan soldiers in the war and histories of each regiment, and an original set of official Civil War records, *The War of the Rebellion: A Compilation of the Official Records of the Union and Confederate Armies*, published by the national government, once owned by General Spalding *(see description under Woodland Cemetery for information on General Spalding)*.

The second floor of the Monroe County Historical Museum features the largest exhibit in the world dedicated to **General George Armstrong Custer**. People from all over the globe, including renowned authors and historians, visit this exhibit.

Personal items once belonging to Custer on display include his christening gown, wedding invitation, family photos, lock of hair, buffalo coat and camp tent, desk from Fort Abraham Lincoln, and his Remington rolling block rifle. Custer was a skilled taxidermist, and the museum exhibits several of his mounted animal heads or relics of the chase.

Civil War items related to Custer include his cavalry saber, personal guidon as commander of the Michigan Cavalry Brigade, period magazines featuring the general on the covers, and a Confederate Bowie knife. Confiscated by Company A of the 4th Michigan Infantry during an encounter with Wheat's Louisiana Tigers at the Battle of New Bridge on the Chickahominy River, members of the 4th presented this unique short sword to General Custer who fought alongside them in the battle.

In all, approximately 20 exhibits are dedicated to Monroe's most famous citizen. The museum occupies the site where the family home of Elizabeth Bacon Custer once stood. *(See entry below)*. A guidebook of General Custer sites in Monroe is available at the museum.

BACON | CUSTER HOME

703 Cass Street | *private residence*

Elizabeth "Libbie" Bacon Custer and her husband George inherited this house upon the death of her father, Judge Bacon. The couple resided in the home whenever they returned to Monroe for short visits and following the Civil War, when Custer was in between military assignments. Originally, the home stood at 126 S. Monroe Street, the current site of the Monroe County Historical Museum. The restored home is the private residence of renowned Custer living historian Steve Alexander and his wife.

OLD FAIRGROUNDS

Noble and Monroe Streets | now a commercial/residential area

The training grounds for three regiments organized in Monroe: 7th Michigan Infantry, 15th Michigan Volunteer Infantry, and 1st Michigan Light Artillery, Battery H. Local resident **John M. Oliver**, colonel of the 15th, later commanded a brigade in General Sherman's army and was brevetted major general.

CUSTER EQUESTRIAN STATUE

Corner of Elm and Monroe Streets

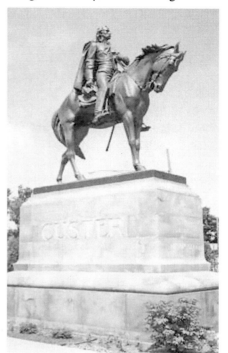

Designed by sculptor Edward Potter, the statue entitled *Sighting the Enemy* depicts **Custer** at the Battle of Gettysburg. Originally unveiled on June 4, 1910, in a ceremony attended by President William Howard Taft and Custer's widow, **Elizabeth Bacon Custer**, a rededication ceremony was held in 2010 to commemorate the statue's 100th anniversary.

The statue first stood in the center of Washington and First Streets, between the First Presbyterian Church where Custer wed hometown girl Libbie Bacon, in what was then dubbed the "wedding of the century," and the courthouse, where Mayor George Spalding, a Civil War brigadier general, gave a public eulogy for Custer and the Monroe men killed at the Battle of the Little Big Horn.

An outline of the statue base is still embedded in the intersection. In 1923, the statue was deemed a traffic hazard and moved to Soldiers and Sailors Park. In 1955, it was moved again to its present location.

LAWRENCE A. FROST COLLECTION OF CUSTERIANA

Ellis Reference and Information Center | Monroe County Library
3700 South Custer St. | (734) 241-5277

The **George Armstrong Custer** Collection at the Monroe County Library System is a multi-media resource center specializing in the life and times of General George Armstrong Custer. A major portion of this collection was acquired by Monroe resident and avid Custer historian, the late **Dr. Lawrence A. Frost**, and continues to grow steadily through additional acquisitions. The collection houses numerous books on the Civil War, Native Americans, and the Custer story; but also maintains a wide variety of maps, photographs, video tapes, slides, sound recordings, paintings, and an extensive subject/vertical file. Color photocopies of Custer's West Point diploma and military commissions signed by Presidents Lincoln and Johnson can also be viewed here.

WHILE GENERAL GEORGE ARMSTRONG CUSTER'S LEGACY is overshadowed by his defeat at the Battle of the Little Big Horn, most people don't realize he was a celebrated Civil War hero who was revered by the men he led.

Major General Phillip Sheridan acknowledged Custer's many contributions to the Union effort by purchasing the writing table upon which the terms of the Confederate surrender were written and presenting it to the general's wife, Libbie, along with this note:

"And permit me to say Madam that there is scarcely an individual in our service who had contributed more to bring about this desirable result than your very gallant husband."

A replica of the table is on exhibit at the Monroe County Historical Museum along with one of the largest Custer exhibits in the world. The original table is at the Smithsonian.

CUSTER FARM

3048 North Custer Road | private residence

George Custer, his brother Nevin, and their wives jointly purchased this 116-acre farm in August of 1871, where Nevin and his family resided. Visitors to the farm included Buffalo Bill Cody and Annie Oakley. Dandy, Custer's favorite horse, was buried in the orchard near the barn. At the Battle of Little Big Horn, Custer met his demise astride his horse Vic. Dandy survived as he was left behind with the pack train. A historic marker stands on the front lawn of the farmhouse.

MARTHA BARKER COUNTRY STORE | FORMER PAPER MILL SCHOOL

3815 North Custer / (734) 240-7780

Monroe is also the hometown of **Colonel Norman Hall** who learned of his acceptance to West Point Military Academy while attending the rural Paper Mill School. After entering the service in 1859, Hall - a 25 year old second lieutenant - witnessed the execution of John Brown and opening shots of the Civil War when Confederate batteries fired upon the Union-held Fort Sumter in April of 1861.

In July 1862, Hall earned the rank of colonel of volunteers and was appointed commander of the 7th Michigan Infantry which served heroically in the West Woods at Antietam. The following December, Hall volunteered his brigade for a dangerous mission that involved crossing the Rappahannock River under heavy enemy fire. Traveling in pontoon boats, the brigade managed to outwit the enemy and reached Fredericksburg where they rid the city of Confederate sharpshooters who impeded the ability of Union engineers to lay pontoon bridges. The mission earned the 7th Michigan the moniker "The Forlorn Hope At Fredericksburg."

Colonel Hall also witnessed the carnage at Gettysburg. During the breach at the "Angle" of the Union line, Hall's troops were among the last remaining Union soldiers to assist in repulsing Pickett's charge, thus saving Union forces from defeat.

Early in his military career, Colonel Hall contracted a regional disease. That disease combined with the continuous hardships of war took its toll on his health. Colonel Hall died on May 26, 1867, at the age of 30.

HISTORIC WOODLAND CEMETERY

East Fourth and Jerome Streets

Established in 1810, Historic Woodland Cemetery is one of Michigan's oldest cemeteries. It's the final resting place of 107 Civil War soldiers as well as influential politicians of this turbulent time.

Henry D. Gale, a sergeant in Company C, of the 5th Michigan Cavalry, died on May 11, 1864, from wounds sustained at the Battle of Yellow Tavern, Virginia. It was during this battle that Confederate General Jeb Stuart was mortally wounded by a 5th Michigan trooper. Two years earlier, Gale's younger brother, **Franklin**, died in action at Malvern Hill, Virginia on July 1, 1862. The brothers are buried next to each other.

Medal of Honor recipient **Peter Sype**, a private in Company B of the 47th Ohio Volunteer Infantry, is buried in the Trinity Lutheran section of the cemetery. Sype earned our nation's highest military honor for demonstrating "gallantry of action" at Vicksburg, Mississippi on May 3, 1863, when he and several volunteers attempted to ram the enemy's batteries with a steam tug and two barges carrying explosives. Although severely wounded in battle in 1864, Sype survived and lived until the age of 82.

Brigadier General Joseph R. Smith, seriously wounded in the Mexican War, offered his services as drill master of Company A, 4th Michigan Infantry, known as the "Smith Guards" in his

honor. He became chief mustering officer for the State of Michigan. Monroe's G.A.R. Post was named after him as well.

Other notables buried at Woodland include:

+ **Brigadier General George W. Spalding** enlisted as a sergeant in the 4th Michigan Infantry and was promoted to lieutenant colonel of the 18th Michigan Infantry and colonel of the 12th Tennessee Cavalry (Union). For his bravery in the Battle of Nashville in 1865, Spalding became a brevet brigadier general. General Spalding, who later became mayor of Monroe and a United States Congressman, is known for his unique attempt to rid Nashville of venereal disease while serving as the city's Provost Marshall.
+ **Dr. Eduard Dorsch** attended President Lincoln's inauguration and served as a surgeon on the U.S. Pension Board.
+ Businessman **William H. Boyd** and Michigan Supreme Court Chief Justice/United States Senator **Isaac P. Christiancy** were founding members of the Republican Party.
+ The Bacon and Custer family plots. Although General Custer and his wife Elizabeth are buried at West Point, family members including George's brother **Boston** and nephew **Autie Reed** are buried here. Both died with General Custer at the Battle of the Little Big Horn on June 25, 1976.
+ **Colonel Ira R. Grosvenor** recruited and organized the 7th Michigan Infantry. He is the brother of Michigan Lieutenant Governor Ebenzer Oliver Grosvenor.
+ *Monroe's Woodland Cemetery Tour*, pamphlet, written by David Ingall identifies the gravesites of prominent Monroe residents buried here. It is available at the Monroe County Historical Museum.

MONROE COUNTY CIVIL WAR SOLDIERS MEMORIAL MONUMENT

East Front St. | *Soldiers and Sailors Park*

This beautiful new memorial listing more than 400 names of those from Monroe County who died in the Civil War will be dedicated in the spring of 2012.

FREDERICK NIMS HOUSE

206 West Noble | *private residence*

This stately Greek revival home built in the 1830s belonged to **Frederick Nims**, aide to General Custer during the Civil War. A first lieutenant in the 5th Michigan Cavalry, Lieutenant Nims was the last surviving officer on General Custer's staff. The home is listed on the National Register of Historic Places and was renamed "Shadowland" in 1914 after undergoing extensive remodeling.

MONROE GOLF AND COUNTRY CLUB

611 Cole Rd. | *Monroe*

The country club was once the home of **Colonel Ira R. Grosvenor** who raised and organized the 7th Michigan Infantry, which trained in Monroe. He led the regiment through the Peninsular Campaign battles in 1862. Colonel Grosvenor named the home "Fair Oaks" because the grounds reminded him of the Virginia terrain where the 1862 battles took place. Legend claims his ghost haunts the upper floor of the building.

Mount Clemens

CLINTON GROVE CEMETERY

21189 Cass Avenue

Brigadier General Henry Dwight Terry, colonel of the 5th Michigan Infantry is buried here. He became a brigade commander and the commandant of Johnson's Island Confederate Prison in Sandusky Bay, Ohio.

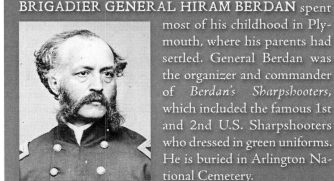

BRIGADIER GENERAL HIRAM BERDAN spent most of his childhood in Plymouth, where his parents had settled. General Berdan was the organizer and commander of *Berdan's Sharpshooters*, which included the famous 1st and 2nd U.S. Sharpshooters who dressed in green uniforms. He is buried in Arlington National Cemetery.

CAMP STOCKTON
South Gratiot and Robertson Street

Training site of the 8th Michigan Cavalry and Battery M, 1st Michigan Light Artillery, extended from this intersection to the Clinton River.

Plymouth

PLYMOUTH HISTORICAL MUSEUM

155 S. Main Street | (734) 455-8940

Civil War exhibits related to Plymouth and Michigan including Company C, 24th Michigan Infantry. Members were recruited in August 1862 at the village green which is now known as Kellogg Park.

The Weldon Petz Abraham Lincoln Collection features artifacts from Lincoln's life including a rare book once belonging to him, family genealogy and photographs, a lock of hair, a life mask circa 1860, hand-written legal documents, law books, Civil War art, and artifacts relating to his assassination.

Dr. Petz acquired over 12,000 Lincoln artifacts, research papers, and resource materials over a period of 70 years making this the largest collection in Michigan, second largest in the Midwest, and one of the finest private collections in the country.

PLYMOUTH COMMUNITY VETERANS MEMORIAL PARK

S. Main and Church Streets

A red brick path winds through this peaceful park lined with monuments paying tribute to veterans of all wars from the city of Plymouth and Plymouth Township. Amidst the other monuments stands a beautiful and unique Civil War monument dedicated to "Those Sons Of Plymouth Who Offered Their Lives In The War Between The States." The monument, a gift of Harry E. Bradner, was originally unveiled in a ceremony on September 9, 1917, in Kellogg Park. The monument was later moved to Riverside Cemetery, where it stood for many years before being moved to its current location at the park.

Pontiac

OAK HILL CEMETERY

216 University Drive

Oak Hill Cemetery is the final resting place of **General Israel B. Richardson** and **Governor Moses Wisner.** Mortally wounded at Antietam, President Lincoln personally visited the injured general. It has been said Lincoln cried upon receiving the news of General Richardson's death. General Richardson was one of the Army of the Potomac's best generals, who may have become its overall commander, had it not been for his unfortunate death.

PROMINENT OFFICERS OF THE 2ND MICHIGAN - The 2nd Michigan Cavalry enjoys the distinction of producing several prominent officers that would go on to become major contributors to the Union cause: Colonel Phillip Sheridan, Colonel Gordon Granger, Major Russell Alger and Major Robert H.G. Minty.

Governor Moses Wisner, the 12th governor of Michigan, organized the 22nd Michigan Infantry which trained at the Pontiac Fair Grounds. Within five months of departing Pontiac with his regiment, the Governor contracted typhoid fever in Kentucky and died. His estate is now home to the Pine Grove Historical Museum.

Also buried here are: **Brigadier General Joseph T. Copeland**, who preceded General G.A. Custer as commander of the Michigan Cavalry Brigade and **Salmon S. Mathews**, lieutenant colonel of the 5th Michigan Infantry. Mathews was severely wounded at the battles of Malvern Hill, Gettysburg and the Wilderness. He was brevetted colonel and brigadier general for gallant and meritorious service in those battles. Also interred here is **Lieutenent Colonel Melvin Brewer**, one of Custer's finest officers, was killed at the Battle of Third Winchester, Virginia, on September 19, 1864, while commanding the 7th Michigan Cavalry.

A cenotaph for **Private John Stevens**, who enlisted in Company G, 54th Massachusettes Infantry (all black regiment) is here. Private Stevens died during the assault on Fort Wagner, South Carolina on July 18, 1863. This action was depicted in the movie *Glory*. He lies on the battlefield in a mass grave which, over time, has been washed into the sea.

PONTIAC CITY HALL

Woodward and Water Streets

Bronze Civil War soldier monument at parade rest.

OLD FAIRGROUNDS

Fairgrove and Saginaw Streets

A carved stone denotes the training site of the 22nd Michigan Infantry, known as Camp Richardson.

PINE GROVE HISTORICAL MUSEUM

405 Cesar Chavez Avenue | (248) 338-6732

The museum is the former estate of Governor Moses Wisner, who was also colonel of the 22nd Michigan Infantry. The museum contains Civil War artifacts.

Port Huron

CIVIL WAR MONUMENT

1104 Grove Avenue

Tall Grand Army of the Republic Civil War monument features two stone carved soldiers at the base along with the original cannons fired during the Siege of Vicksburg in Mississippi and a standard bearer on top.

LAKESIDE CEMETERY

3663 10th Avenue

William Sanborn, lieutenant colonel of the 22nd Michigan Infantry is buried here. He was brevetted colonel and brigadier general for "conspicuous gallantry at the battle of Chickamauga and meritorious service during the war." The Port Huron GAR Post was named after him.

William Hartsuff, captain in the 10th Michigan Infantry and lieutenant colonel/assistant inspector general in the Army of the Ohio is also interred here. He was brevetted brigadier general of the United State Volunteers, on January 24, 1865. He and his two brothers all became Civil War generals.

Stockbridge

STOCKBRIDGE TOWN HALL

123 South Clinton

A nice example of a Civil War soldier monument at parade rest and a Dalgreen cannon are on display. In the town hall basement is a large period print of the infamous Andersonville Prison in Georgia, where many Union soldiers were imprisoned and endured horrendous treatment.

Tecumseh

BROOKSIDE CEMETERY

501 North Union Street

The Civil War monument, erected in 1882 as a tribute to the war's veterans, was moved to the entrance of Brookside Cemetery in 1928. The cemetery is the final resting place for several Civil War soldiers including **Captain Elliot Grey**, a member of the 7th Michigan Cavalry under General Custer's command, whom the General entrusted to care for his prized horse Don Juan when he was on assignment after the Civil War.

    Rhoda Wells Pitts Bacon, stepmother to Elizabeth Bacon Custer, is buried in Brookside Cemetery alongside her first husband.

DON JUAN'S GRAVE

West Russell Road and South Occidental | *private property*

Tecumseh is the burial site of General Custer's horse **Don Juan**. Custer had bequeathed his prized horse to Captain Elliot Grey. The horse became famous after bolting forward near the review stand during the Grand Review parade in Washington, D.C. at the end of the Civil War - taking the spotlight momentarily off the president and other important officials and on to the dashing young general. Custer, who ironically was an excellent horseman, attributed this mishap to the horse being spooked when a young girl attempted to put a wreath around its neck.

TECUMSEH MUSEUM

302 East Chicago Boulevard | *(517) 423-2374*

Civil War items of interest.

Tipton

FRANKLIN CEMETERY

North Tipton Highway | *1/4 mile North of M-50*

Dedicated on July 4, 1866, this flag draped obelisk is the first Michigan monument erected to honor Civil War veterans and lists the names of those from the Tipton area who died during the war.

Ypsilanti

YPSILANTI HISTORICAL MUSEUM

220 North Huron Street | *(734) 482-4990*

Civil War artifacts are displayed

HIGHLAND CEMETERY

943 North River Street

Brigadier General Byron M. Cutcheon, colonel of the 20th Michigan Infantry and brigade commander is buried here. General Cutcheon was awarded the Medal of Honor for leading his regiment in a charge against the enemy at Horseshoe Bend, Kentucky on May 10, 1863.

    Brigadier General Justus McKinstry is buried here in the family plot. The West Point graduate was appointed U.S. Quartermaster and Provost Marshall of St. Louis but later was arrested for alleged corruption and fraud. Charges were dropped upon his resignation.

The Ypsilanti Civil War Memorial is located at the south end of the cemetery. Erected by Mary Ann Starkweather and the Woman's Relief Corps of Ypsilanti, the statue was unveiled on Memorial Day in 1895 and dedicated:

"...in memory of the men who in the War of the Great Rebellion fought to uphold their country's flag. They died to make their country free."

THOMPSON BLOCK

404-413 River Street

Initially called the Norris Block after its builder Mark Norris, an Ypsilanti pioneer, this Italianate three-story building designed for residential and retail use played a prominent role in Ypsilanti history. Completed in 1861, the building served as barracks for the 14th Michigan Infantry in 1862 when they were mustered into service in February of that year. According to early newspaper accounts, the Norris Block barracks was a comfortable and fun dwelling that offered a basement kitchen where each company prepared their own food and rooms on the upper floors to host dances and spirited debates. The 14th Michigan remained at the Norris Block barracks for two months. In 1863, the Norris Block was again used for training by the 27th Michigan Infantry. Throughout the years, the building was used for many different commercial ventures. Recent plans were underway to convert the building into luxury residential lofts and retail space when a 2009 fire caused major damage.

GRAND ARMY OF THE REPUBLIC HALL, CARPENTER POST #180

108 Pearl Street

Original meeting site of Civil War Veterans Carpenter Post #180 and Women's Relief Corps #65 of Ypsilanti.

HARRIET TUBMAN STATUE

229 West Michigan Avenue | plaza adjacent to the library

This bronze, life-like statue of **Harriet Tubman** leading a child pays tribute to this remarkable woman, an escaped slave who in turn led others to freedom as a conductor on the Underground Railroad. It serves as a testament to the area's rich abolition and Underground Railroad history.

Dubbed the "Moses of her people," this suffragist and humanitarian became the first woman to command an armed military raid. In June 1863, she guided Colonel James Montgomery and his 2nd South Carolina black regiment up the Combahee River where they took overwhelmed Confederate outposts, destroyed stockpiles of cotton, food and weapons, and liberated over 700 slaves.

STATE OF MICHIGAN'S MILITARY CONTRIBUTION TO THE CIVIL WAR

Thirty-one infantry regiments; eleven cavalry; one engineers and mechanics; one sharpshooters; fourteen batteries of light artillery and several companies in other state and U.S. regular army regiments.

THE 1ST MICHIGAN ENGINEERS AND MECHANICS were

the backbone of General Sherman's army building fortifications, roads, and bridges during the Atlanta Campaign, "March to the Sea" and Carolina Campaign.

CIVIL WAR ARMY ORGANIZATION

ARMY
2-4 Corps / 108,000 Soldiers

CORPS
2-4 Divisions / 36,000 Soldiers

DIVISION
3-4 Brigades / 12,000 Soldiers

BRIGADE
3-6 Regiments / 4,000 Soldiers

REGIMENT
10 Companies / 1,000 Soldiers

COMPANY
100 Soldiers

VETERANS' CEMETERY

In April 1886, the Board of Managers of the Michigan Veterans' Facility set aside five acres for a cemetery. The Grand Rapids Post of the Grand Army of the Republic dedicated the cemetery on Memorial Day, May 31, 1886. The original cemetery was designed in the form of a Maltese cross with 262 grave sites in each of its four sections. In 1894 a granite statue of a Civil War soldier was placed at the center of the cross. By the time of its centennial in 1986, the cemetery had recorded over 4,000 burials of veterans and

---

JOSEPH E BRANDLE
MEDAL OF HONOR
CLR SGT CO C
17 MICH INF

OCT 8 1839
MAY 13 1909

SOUTHWEST MICHIGAN

2

Southwest Michigan also provided excellent soldiers and leadership to the Union cause as well as vocal opposition to the repulsive institution of slavery. Grand Rapids' **Major General Byron Root Pierce**, colonel of the 3rd Michigan Infantry and brigade commander, was seriously wounded at Gettysburg. This did not stop him, however, from becoming a division commander and one of Michigan's best citizen soldiers.

Grand Rapids' **Major General Russell A. Alger**, colonel of the 5th Michigan Cavalry, who led them gallantly at Gettysburg, became governor of Michigan, U.S. Senator, U.S. Secretary of War, and National Commander-in-Chief of the Grand Army of the Republic.

Sturgis' Major **General William L. Stoughton**, colonel of the 11th Michigan Infantry, whose brigade staunchly defended "Snodgrass Hill" at the Battle of Chickamauga and thus helped save the Union Army.

Under the command of Allegan's **Benjamin D. Pritchard**, lieutenant colonel of the 4th Michigan Cavalry, Confederate President Jefferson Davis was tracked down and captured. The lieutenant colonel was brevetted brigadier general for this action.

Although the 25th Michigan was outnumbered ten to one, their commander, Schoolcraft's Colonel Orlando H. Moore, refused to surrender on Independence Day. The 25th Michigan stood their ground and defeated Brigadier General John Hunt Morgan's Confederate cavalry on July 4, 1863 at the Battle of Tebb's Bend, Kentucky.

Abolitionists in southwest Michigan welcomed freedom seekers arriving from southern and western states into their communities or helped them continue their journey eastward to Detroit and across the river to Canada. History has not forgotten the determination of the abolitionists and freedom seekers. The largest memorial in the nation commemorating the Underground Railroad and the quest for freedom is located in Battle Creek, home of escaped slave Sojourner Truth – who became an influential abolitionist and women's rights activist during the 19th century. The southwest community of Vandalia became known as the "hotbed of abolition" due to the large amount of anti-slavery activity that took place here.

Albion
RIVERSIDE CEMETERY
1301 South Superior Street

William Henry Harrison Beadle, lieutenant colonel of the 1st Michigan Sharpshooters, is interred here. After being severely wounded in battle, which forced him to resign his officer's commission, Lieutenant Colonel Beadle rejoined the army in the Veterans Reserve Corps and was brevetted a brigadier general on March 13, 1865.

After the war, he became the Dakota Territory Superintendent of Public Instruction where he championed the "school lands program" to fund public education. He also served as president of the Madison State Normal School in South Dakota. A statue of General Beadle in the U.S. Capitol rotunda states, "He saved the School Lands."

GAR monument with bronze tablet listing the names of the members of the E. W. Hollingsworth Post #210 stands here.

Allegan
OLD JAIL MUSEUM
113 Walnut Street | (269) 673-8292

Civil War artifacts including personal items of **Brigadier General Benjamin Dudley Pritchard** *(see Oakwood Cemetery entry below for more on Pritchard).*

GENERAL BENJAMIN PRITCHARD HOUSE
330 Davis Street | private residence

This home was once the family residence of **General Benjamin Pritchard.**

ALLEGAN CIVIL WAR MEMORIAL
113 Chestnut Street

An impressive Civil War soldier monument of a flag bearer with drawn sword stands outside the Allegan County Courthouse.

OAKWOOD CEMETERY
Western Avenue (M-89)

Brigadier General Benjamin D. Pritchard, lieutenant colonel of the 4th Michigan Cavalry is interred here. As commander of the 4th, he led his men in the capture of the fleeing Confederate President Jefferson Davis at Irwinville, Georgia on May 10, 1865. Also buried here is **Brigadier General Elisha Mix**, colonel of the 8th Michigan Cavalry.

Allen
ALLEN TOWNSHIP CEMETERY
700 Edon Road | south of U.S.-12

A Civil War soldier monument at parade rest is here as well as the grave of **Captain William G. Whitney** of the 11th Michigan Infantry. Captain Whitney received the Medal of Honor for actions at the Battle of Chickamauga on September 20, 1863 where he, a second lieutenant, went out among the dead and wounded enemy to retrieve their cartridge boxes containing much needed ammuni-

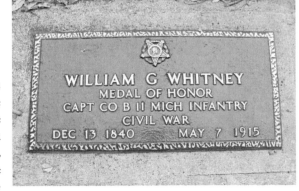

tion. He and his comrades used the confiscated ammunition to repulse the Confederate attack.

Battle Creek
SOLDIERS AND SAILORS MONUMENT
Monument Square | intersection of East Michigan and Washington Avenues and Van Buren Street

Dedicated in 1901, the 35 foot Soldiers and Sailors monument features two bronze soldiers atop a granite pillar carrying the American flag.

UNDERGROUND RAILROAD SCULPTURE

1 East Michigan Avenue

Standing 14 feet high and 28 feet long, this monument is the nation's largest tribute to the Underground Railroad. An Ed Dwight design (he designed the Gateway to Freedom monument in Detroit as well as other national monuments of prominent African Americans), this bronze statue depicts abolitionist **Harriet Tubman**, known as the "Black Moses," and local Underground Railroad conductors **Erastus and Sarah Hussey**, leading a group of freedom seekers to safety.

Built by the W. K. Kellogg Foundation, the massive monument honors the brave men and women who demonstrated moral fortitude by leading or housing refugees in their journey to freedom despite severe consequences including hefty fines, injury, death or imprisonment. It also pays tribute to those who embarked on this treacherous journey amidst an uncertain future in search of the coveted ideals of liberty and freedom.

SOJOURNER TRUTH STATUE

Monument Park at the end of Sojourner Truth Downtown Parkway

Once buried in an unmarked grave, this dramatic outdoor testament pays tribute to a remarkable woman far ahead of her time. A 12-foot, bronze statue designed by sculptor Tina Allen honors the outspoken anti-slavery and women's rights activist. The bold monument, framed by the First United Methodist Church and city hall, takes center stage in the large plaza that features an amphitheater and meandering stonewalls. Two quotations by this inspirational woman can be found on bronze plaques.

SOJOURNER TRUTH INSTITUTE | HERITAGE BATTLE CREEK RESEARCH CENTER

165 North Washington

The Sojourner Truth Institute was established to expand the historical and biographical knowledge of Sojourner Truth's life work and carry on her mission by educating others and supporting projects that reflect the ideals and principles for which she stood. The Battle Creek Research Center houses one of the most extensive archives of Sojourner Truth artifacts and records in the United States.

OAK HILL CEMETERY

255 South Avenue

Born into slavery in New York, **Sojourner Truth**, a well-known abolitionist and women's rights activist, is buried here. She escaped slavery with her infant daughter in 1826, and later went to court to recover her son, becoming the first black woman to win this type of case against a white man.

Truth toured the country speaking out against slavery, helped recruit black soldiers into the Union army, and provided aid to freed slaves. Prior to the Civil War, she moved to Michigan.

Also buried here are: **Sergeant Charles M. Holton** of Company A, 7th Michigan Cavalry who earned the Medal of Honor for capturing the flag of the 55th Virginia Infantry at Falling Waters, Virginia on July 14, 1863.

Medal of Honor recipient **Edward Van Winkle**, Sergeant of the 145th New York Infantry, Company C. Sergeant Van Winkle earned his medal for taking an advanced position along the skirmish line and charging the enemy, driving them from their cannons.

Erastus Hussey, a Quaker, an ardent abolitionist, was stationmaster on the Underground Railroad, who according to his personal estimation, assisted 1,000 people in their journey to freedom. When asked in later years if stationmasters received pay, the editor of the antislavery publication, *Michigan Liberty Press*, claimed: "We were working for humanity." Hussey was mayor of Battle Creek and a state representative and senator. He attended the "Under the Oaks" meeting in Jackson where the Republican Party was founded.

Centreville
PRAIRIE RIVER CEMETERY
N. Nottowa Street

A unique Civil War monument with a granite base features a soldier holding his gun in his left hand while shielding his eyes with his right hand as if he were scanning the battlefield.

Coldwater
OAK GROVE CEMETERY
West Chicago Street and U.S.-12

A tall memorial pays tribute to Company B of the 44th Illinois Infantry made up of men from Coldwater and surrounding towns.

The final resting place of several Civil War veterans including: **Major General Clinton C. Fisk,** the founder of Nashville, Tennessee's Fisk University; **Brigadier General John G. Parkhurst,** originally Colonel of the 9th Michigan Infantry; and Medal of Honor recipient **Joseph E. Brandle.**

Brandle, a private in Company C, 17th Michigan Infantry was cited for his bravery at the battle at Lenoire, Tennessee on November 16, 1863. His citation reads: "While color bearer of his regiment, having twice been wounded and the sight of one eye destroyed, still held to the colors until ordered to the rear by his regimental commander."

Historic markers in Coldwater denote the Fisk and Parkhurst family homesteads.

Colonel Henry Clarke Gilbert of the 19th Michigan Infantry is also buried at Oak Grove. Colonel Gilbert was mortally wounded during the Battle of Resaca, dying on May 24, 1864.

A memorial stone in the Harrington family plot at Oak Grove Cemetery is dedicated to **Lieutenant Henry Harrington.** Commander of Company C of the 7th U.S. Cavalry, part of Lt. Col. George A. Custer's troops. This West Point graduate died at the Battle of the Little Big Horn in Montana on June 25, 1876. His body was never identified and lies on the battlefield. Lakota and Cheyenne eyewitness battle accounts describe the actions of one cavalryman whom they called the "bravest man they ever fought." Many believe Lt. Harrington is the "bravest man" to whom they refer.

Old Sam, one of two hundred horses supplied to the famous Loomis Battery which was involved in 12 battles including the

LOCAL TOWN SUPPLIED HORSES TO UNION EFFORT ⋅ Prior to the advent of the automobile, Coldwater was known nationally and internationally for its horses. During the Civil War, the Union relied heavily on this area to supply the war effort with much needed draft and cavalry horses used to move troops and equipment.

bloody battle at Chickamauga, is buried here too. Sam, who pulled streetcars prior to being called into war service, was a favorite among the troops.

Although wounded several times, Sam was the only one of the two hundred horses used by the Loomis Battery to survive and mustered out in 1865. Upon his return to Coldwater, he was met at the depot by hundreds of citizens and given a hero's welcome.

When old Sam died in November 1876 at the ripe old age of 27, fellow battery members snuck the dead horse into the cemetery after sundown and buried him with full honors including taps. Although Sam's burial was secretive, a marker now denotes his grave.

FOUR CORNERS (LOOMIS) PARK
U.S.-27 & U.S.-12

An original 10-pound Parrott rifled cannon from the Loomis Battery A, 1st Michigan Light Artillery, originating in Coldwater is located here. Commemorative plaques list all the members of this battery. A plaque also honors Old Sam, a faithful horse that served the battery.

Across the street, next to the library, stands a Civil War soldier monument at parade rest.

PARKHURST HOMESTEAD
55 North Clay Street | private residence

The former home of General John Parkhurst.

OLD FAIRGROUNDS
State and Marshall Streets

The training site for Michigan Light Artillery Batteries: A (Loomis), F, L, and 9th Michigan Cavalry.

HOME DEPOT
U.S.-12 | near I-69

Former location of the large horse farm where many horses sold to the Union army were raised.

Dowagiac

MUSEUM OF SOUTHWESTERN MICHIGAN COLLEGE
58900 Cherry Grove Road | (269) 782-1374

The museum features an Underground Railroad and Cass County in the Civil War exhibit.

CIVIL WAR MONUMENT | BURKE PARK
Main, Lowe and Spruce Streets

This impressive Civil War memorial features five individually carved stone soldiers representing the three branches of the Civil War army, the navy and a standard bearer at the top.

MCKINELY ELEMENTARY SCHOOL
First and Paris Avenues

Sight of Camp Willcox where the 19th Michigan Infantry organized and trained before going off to war in September 1862.

Galesburg

SHAFTER MONUMENT

M-96 and Michigan Avenue | *downtown*

This bust statue with a granite base immortalizes Civil War **Brigadier General William R. Shafter.** 1st Lieutenant in the 7th Michigan Infantry, he was awarded the Medal of Honor for heroism in leading a charge during the Battle of Fair Oaks. Shafter served as a major in the 19th Michigan Infantry and colonel of the 17th U.S. Colored Troops. Later he fought in the Indian Wars and was promoted to major general in command of U.S. expeditionary forces in Cuba during the Spanish American War.

WILLIAM RUFUS SHAFTER

Grand Rapids

GRAND RAPIDS HOME FOR VETERANS *(formerly Michigan Soldiers Home)* AND CEMETERY

3000 Monroe NE

On a national level, the Civil War left an estimated half million veterans disabled from wounds or disease. When a proposed federal plan failed to materialize, Michigan chose to honor a debt to its wartime veterans by opening a state home for those in need. Passed by the Michigan Legislature and signed by **Governor Russell A. Alger** *(see Elmwood Cemetery entry)*, Public Act 152 of 1885 established a home for disabled soldiers, sailors and marines.

In 1886, five acres of the property was set aside for use as a cemetery. The Grand Rapids Post of the Grand Army of the Republic dedicated the cemetery on Memorial Day, 1886. In 1894, the cemetery's fountain and statue of a Civil War soldier were completed as a tribute to the Civil War veterans buried here. These are the only remaining structures from that period.

Seaman Franklin L. Wilcox and **Brigadier General Frederick S. Hutchinson** are buried here. Wilcox was awarded the Medal of Honor for bravery exhibited on January 15, 1865, when he jumped onto the beach from the U.S.S. Minnesota and assaulted North Carolina's Fort Fisher. At nightfall, he helped bring back the

wounded as well as the ship's colors. General Hutchinson was colonel of the 15th Michigan Infantry.

FULTON STREET CEMETERY

791 E. Fulton Street

Brigadier General Stephen G. Chaplin, Brigadier General William P. Innes and **Major General Byron Root Pierce** are buried here. General Chaplin died in January 1864 as a result of a lingering hip wound received in 1862 at the Battle of Fair Oaks, Virginia. General Innes was colonel of the 1st Michigan Engineers and Mechanics, one of the best engineering regiments in General William T. Sherman's army.

Major General Pierce was seriously wounded on July 2, 1863, while leading his brigade, including the 3rd Michigan Infantry, in the Peach Orchard during the Battle of Gettysburg.

One of Michigan's outstanding "citizen soldiers," Major General Pierce served as commandant of the Michigan Soldiers Home and was the last surviving Michigan Civil War general.

Also buried here is **Major Peter Weber**, another fine officer in the the Michigan Cavalry Brigade, who was killed leading a charge of the 6th Michigan Cavalry at the Battle of Falling Waters, Maryland, on July 14, 1863.

GRAND RAPIDS PUBLIC MUSEUM

272 Pearl Street NW | (616) 929-1700

Many Civil War artifacts are on display at the museum including the frock coat of **Brigadier General Stephen G. Champlin** and his sword, as well as artifacts belonging to **Major General Byron Root Pierce**.

KENT COUNTY CIVIL WAR SOLDIERS MONUMENT

Division and Monroe Avenues

Located in the park is a unique zinc memorial. It was recently restored reflecting its original grandeur and now includes plaques outlining the monument's history as well as Kent County's role in the Civil War.

OAK HILL CEMETERY

647 Hall Street SE

In this cemetery stands the Custer Post GAR monument and burial area. **Brigadier General Israel C. Smith**, a West Point graduate and colonel of the 10th Michigan Cavalry, is one notable buried here. As a captain in the 3rd Michigan Infantry, Smith was commended for his gallantry during the Battle of Gettysburg where he was wounded.

ST. MARK'S EPISCOPAL CHURCH

134 North Division Avenue

A memorial plaque is dedicated to those parishoners who died in the Civil War, including **Major Peter Weber**.

LINCOLN PARK

398 Garfield Avenue NW

A bust monument of **Abraham Lincoln** can be found in the park.

GERALD R. FORD JOB CORPS CENTER

110 Hall Street SE

On the former site of Grand Rapids South High School stands a boulder with the inscription: "Cantonment Anderson". This tribute to the 3rd Michigan Volunteer Infantry rests on the site of the regiment's original muster in May 1861.

First dedicated in a reunion of surviving regiment members held in 1911, the boulder was rededicated in a memorial ceremony in June 2011; two days shy of the regiment's 150-year departure anniversary. An informational tablet was unveiled at the recent rededication detailing the history of the spot and the men who left there to fight and die in the war.

The 3rd Michigan organized into companies on 40 acres at the Kent County Agricultural Fairgrounds along Kalamazoo Plank Road, now South Division Avenue. Amidst swamp-like conditions, soldiers drilled on a race track and bunked in a smelly two-story hall where bedding made from straw was a far cry from the comforts of home such as feather comforters or handmade quilts.

At 1,040 men strong, the 3rd Michigan saw action in a dozen campaigns including the First and Second Battles at Bull Run, Fredericksburg, Chancellorsville, The Wilderness, Spotsylvania, Cold Harbor, Petersburg, Appomattox and Gettysburg.

The regiment was commanded by **Colonel Stephen Champlin**, who took command when **Colonel Daniel McConnell** resigned. The 3rd's men disbanded mid-war when the remaining men were absorbed into the 5th Michigan regiment.

Nearly one quarter of the 3rd Michigan died in service. Many soldiers were captured by the Confederacy and became prisoners of war. **Benjamin K. Morse** (*see Lowell*) and **Walter L. Mundell** (*see St. Johns*) were awarded Congressional Medals of Honor.

Cantonment Anderson was named in honor of **Major Robert Anderson**, the commander and defender of South Carolina's Fort Sumter. The 8th Michigan Infantry, 2nd Michigan Cavalry and 1st Michigan Light Artillery, Battery K trained here as well.

CENTRAL HIGH SCHOOL

421 Fountain Street NE

A bronze plaque and boulder denotes the site of Camp Kellogg and Camp Lee, once located where Central High School now stands. The 6th and 7th Michigan Cavalry, part of the famed Michigan Cavalry Brigade led by **General George A. Custer**, trained here. The 10th Michigan Cavalry trained and organized here as well.

Hastings

HISTORIC CHARLTON PARK VILLAGE AND MUSEUM

2545 South Charlton Park Road | (269) 945-3775

Civil War artifacts are on display.

TYDEN PARK

304 North Broadway

A tall Civil War soldier monument at parade rest is located here.

RIVERSIDE CEMETERY

1003 West State Road

Interred here is **Brigadier General William H. Dickey**. Dickey joined the 6th Michigan Infantry as a first lieutenant, and later become the colonel of the 84th U.S. Colored Troops, leading them in the Red River Campaign.

Holland

HOLLAND MUSEUM

31 West 10th Street | (616) 392-9084

Civil War artifacts are on display.

CENTENNIAL PARK

10th and River Streets

The Holland Area War Dead monument located at Centennial Park pays tribute to those from the Holland area who died in all American conflicts including the Civil War.

GENERAL'S FAMOUS RIDE ASTRIDE MICHIGAN-BRED MORGAN - Reinzi, the celebrated black Morgan horse ridden by General Phillip Sheridan during the Battle of Cedar Creek in Virginia, was raised in Michigan and gifted to the General by members of the 2nd Michigan Cavalry. After the famous ride immortalized by the Thomas Buchanan Read poem "Sheridan's Ride," the horse's name was changed to Winchester. Upon his death, Winchester was preserved and is on display at the Smithsonian.

PILGRIM HOME CEMETERY

370 East 16th Street

A Civil War soldier monument at parade rest honors those who served.

Kalamazoo

CAMP SITE OF THE 25TH MICHIGAN VOLUNTEER INFANTRY

Egleston Avenue (Two blocks east of Portage Street)

Boulder with bronze plaque reads: "This stone, placed here on October 1923 by the surviving members of the Twenty-fifth Michigan Volunteer Infantry who served in the Civil War, marks the spot where the regiment went into camp, September 22, 1862."

CAMP FREMONT

Portage Street and Stockbridge Avenue

Location where the 6th Michigan Infantry organized and trained in August of 1861. The site was an old racetrack known as the National Driving Park.

KALAMAZOO VALLEY MUSEUM

230 North Rose Street | (269) 373-7990

Collections contain the uniform and field desk of Schoolcraft native **Colonel Orlando H. Moore** of the 25th Michigan Infantry.

Colonel Moore, the hero of the Battle of Tebbs Bend, Kentucky, who refused to surrender to a much larger Confederate Cavalry force led by Brigadier General John Hunt Morgan on the 4th of July.

BRONSON PARK

South Park Street (downtown)

Abraham Lincoln made only one Michigan appearance. On August 27, 1856, Lincoln visited Kalamazoo where he gave a speech for Republican presidential candidate John C. Freemont.

A GAR boulder with descriptive plate marks the spot where Lincoln stood during his speech.

A Civil War era naval cannon is on display in the park and another commemorative boulder salutes the 11th Michigan Cavalry which trained and organized at Kalamazoo in 1863.

MOUNTAIN HOME CEMETERY

1402 W. Main Street

Brigadier General Dwight May, colonel of the 12th Michigan Infantry and Michigan's lieutenant governor from 1867 to 1869 is buried here. Also buried here is **Charles E. Smith**, lieutenant colonel of the 11th Michigan Cavalry who was brevetted a brigadier general for faithful and meritorious service during the war.

RIVERSIDE CEMETERY

1015 Gull Road

Civil War soldier monument at parade rest is located here.

Lowell

OAKWOOD CEMETERY

301 East Main Street

Buried here is **Corporal Benjamin Morse** of the 3rd Michigan Infantry. He was awarded the Medal of Honor for capturing the flag of the 4th Georgia Battery on May 12, 1864 during the Battle of Spotsylvania, Virginia.

A monument depicting a young Civil War soldier and cannon can be found in the cemetery.

Marshall

GRAND ARMY OF THE REPUBLIC HALL

402 East Marshall | (269) 781-8544

One of the few remaining GAR halls, it was built in 1902 for the Marshall Chapter of the Union Civil War Veterans. The attractive red brick building now houses the Marshall Historic Society's archives and artifacts from the Civil War, Spanish American War, World War I and II along with other Marshall memorabilia. Built at a cost of $3,000, this hall was named for Marshall's Corporal Calvin Colegrove, color-bearer for the Michigan First Infantry, who was killed at the First Battle of Bull Run on July 21, 1861.

A boulder and plaque in front of the GAR Hall marks the site of Camp Owen where the 1st Michigan Engineers & Mechanics organized and trained.

OAKRIDGE CEMETERY

614 Homer Road

Another Michigan hero at Gettysburg is buried here. **Lieutenant George A. Woodruff**, commander of Battery I, First U.S. Artillery, died in battle on July 3, 1863, courageously directing the fire of his cannons during Pickett's Charge.

Adam Crosswhite, an escaped slave who settled in Marshall is interred here. Mr. Crosswhite, along with his wife Sarah and children, moved to Marshall in 1843 after escaping from a Kentucky plantation. Marshall, with its strong anti-slavery sentiment, was part of the Underground Railroad and a hospitable place for blacks to settle. Even at this time, the local school was racially integrated.

In 1847, Kentuckian Francis Giltner, claiming legal ownership of the Crosswhites, sent agents to arrest and retrieve the family. Neighbors were alerted and a town resolution passed to arrest the agents. A historic marker on U.S. 12 marks the spot of this event.

While the agents were jailed and tried for assault, battery and housebreaking, the Crosswhites escaped to Canada. Mr. Giltner sued the leaders behind the agents' arrests and won. Banker, Charles T. Gorham, was determined the sole defendant and fined $4800. Detroit businessman and abolitionist, Zachariah Chandler, paid the fine. *(See Elmwood Cemetery listing in Detroit for more on Chandler).*

New Buffalo

NEW BUFFALO WELCOME CENTER

Interstate 94 near state line

Amidst the numerous historical markers in this vicinity stands one that pays tribute to the Iron Brigade and 24th Michigan Infantry. *(See Detroit entry for more details).*

Niles

Fort St. Joseph Museum

508 E. Main Street | (269) 683-4702

Hand drawn pictographs by **Lakota Chief Sitting Bull** are on display. The pictographs include events in his life which occurred during the Civil War period.

Silverbrook Cemetery

1400 East Main Street

Major General Henry A. Morrow is interred here. As colonel of the famed 24th Michigan Infantry, he courageously led the regiment at McPhearson Woods during the first day of the Battle of Gettysburg, buying the Union Army much needed time. The 24th took the highest casualty rate of any regiment at Gettysburg (80%), and Colonel Morrow would be severely wounded. He recovered to command a brigade, and would stay in the regular army after the war, commanding the 21st U.S. Infantry. General Morrow's brother-in-law, **Colonel Frank Graves**, of the 8th Michigan Infantry, is also buried here. Colonel Graves was taken prisoner at the Battle of the Wilderness and murdered by his captors over his fancy boots.

12th Michigan Infantry Training Site

720 South 11th Street

A supermarket stands near the location of Camp Barker where the 12th Michigan Infantry organized and trained before heading off to the Battle of Shiloh in early 1862.

Saranac

SARANAC CEMETERY

David Highway

Brigadier General Ambrose A. Stevens, colonel of the 21st Michigan Infantry, is buried here. Seriously wounded at the Battle of Perryville, Kentucky on July 25, 1862, Colonel Stevens was made a brevet brigadier general for gallant and meritorious service.

Sturgis

OAKLAWN CEMETERY

300 South Street

Major General William L. Stoughton, colonel of the 11th Michigan infantry who later became a United States congressman, is interred at Oaklawn. General Stoughton led a brigade in the defense of "Snodgrass Hill" at Chickamauga. The final resting place of **Phillip Schlachter**, a member of the 73rd New York Infantry, can also be found here. Schlachter was awarded the Medal of Honor for capturing the flag of the 15th Louisiana infantry on May 12, 1864, during the Battle of Spotsylvania.

Sunfield

GRAND ARMY OF THE REPUBLIC HALL

115 Main Street

The **Samuel W. Grinnell** Post #283 is the only GAR hall in Michigan that has remained in continuous service. Today, it is used by the Sons of Union Veterans, Curtenius Guard Camp #17.

Three Rivers

BOWMAN PARK

East Hoffman and North Main Streets

Tall Civil War soldier monument at parade rest with the names of the battles that area soldiers served in engraved on the base is located here.

RIVERSIDE CEMETERY

Evans Street and Fourth Avenue

John Ayers of the 8th Missouri Infantry is buried here. He received the Medal of Honor for gallantry in a charge at Vicksburg, Mississippi, on May 22, 1863.

SCIDMORE PARK

Michigan and Spring Streets

Pre-Civil War smoothbore cannon used by the local militia is on display here along with a sign describing the cannon's history.

Union City

RIVERSIDE CEMETERY

North Broadway Street

Brigadier General George S. Acker is buried here. General Acker enlisted as captain in the 1st Michigan Cavalry and progressed to Colonel of the 9th Michigan Cavalry. This regiment was instrumental in chasing down Brigadier General John Hunt Morgan and his Confederate Raiders in southeastern Ohio. He was part of Sherman's "March to the Sea" and through the Carolinas.

SOLDIER MONUMENT

Main Street

A nice Civil War soldier monument at parade rest stands next to the church.

Vandalia

MILO BARNES PARK

M-60 west of Main Street

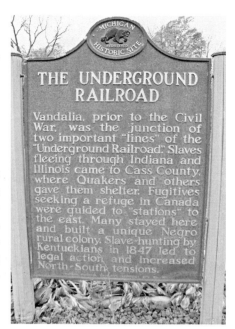

Underground Railroad State of Michigan historical marker stands at the site of O'Dell's Mill where slave catchers and local abolitionsists met in a confrontation during the "Kentucky Raid" of 1847. The result of the action by local abolitionists led to the implementation of a stringent fugitive slave law in 1850 which became one of the catalysts that led to the Civil War. Attached to the marker is a box containing driving guides featuring Cass County Underground Railroad sites. The Vandalia area was known as the "hotbed of abolitionism".

BONINE HOME AND CARRIAGE HOUSE

M-60 and Penn Road

Home of Quaker abolitionist James E. Bonine, the carriage house is a documented station on the Underground Railroad. Both buildings are being restored by the Underground Railroad Society of Cass County.

White Pigeon

WHITE PIGEON TRAIN DEPOT

South St. Joseph Street

Boulder and bronze plaque erected in 1915 once marked the site where the 11th Michigan Infantry and Church's Battery D, 1st Michigan Light Artillery encamped and trained.

THE FAMOUS FARNSWORTH HOUSE INN IN GETTYSBURG is named in memory of Elon John Farnsworth who was killed at Gettysburg during an ill-advised charge. Born in Livingston County's Green Oak Township, Farnsworth was the nephew of John F. Farnsworth, a prominent politician and Civil War general.

Prior to joining the service, Farnsworth was a student at the University of Michigan. He was expelled when a classmate died after being tossed out of a window during a fraternity party.

At the outbreak of the Civil War, Farnsworth was appointed a first lieutenant with the 8th Illinois Cavalry and served with distinction throughout the early years of the war. On June 29, 1863, just two days before the Battle of Gettysburg, Captain Farnsworth was one of three young captains to receive an unexpected promotion in rank to brigadier general by Brigadier General Alfred A. Pleasonton. (George Custer and Wesley Merritt were the other two).

On July 3, just days after his promotion, Brigadier General Farnsworth was ordered to make a charge with his cavalry brigade against Confederate positions below Little Round Top. Although General Farnsworth objected, claiming there was no hope of success, he agreed when the commanding general (Judson "Kilcavalry" Kilpatrick) accused him of cowardice. The entrenched Confederates repulsed the charge. Farnsworth's brigade sustained heavy losses, and the young brigadier general received numerous wounds and died needlessly on the battlefield. He is buried in Rockton, Illinois.

AUTHORS' TOP 10 STATE CIVIL WAR MONUMENTS

1. *Muskegon Soldiers and Sailors Monument in Hackley Park*
2. *Detroit Soldiers and Sailors Monument in Campus Martius Park*
3. *Battle Creek Soldiers and Sailors Monument in Monument Square*
4. *Lansing First Michigan Sharpshooters Monument in Capitol Square*
5. *Jackson "In Defense of the Flag" Statue in Withington Park*
6. *Dowagiac Soldiers and Sailors Monument in Burke Park*
7. *Grand Rapids "Zinc" Soldiers and Sailors Monument at Division and Monroe Avenues Park*
8. *Grand Rapids Soldier Statue in the Soldier's Home Cemetery*
9. *Ionia Soldier Statue on the courthouse lawn*
10. *Corunna "Flag Draped" Memorial on the courthouse lawn*

MID/NORTHERN MICHIGAN

3

When Petoskey-born author **Bruce Catton** released his popular Civil War trilogy in the 1960s, his books captured the imagination and heart of a new generation. In fact, many Civil War buffs today trace their life-long interest in this definitive American event back to early encounters as children to the spellbinding pages of Catton's books. The inspiration behind these books came from the tales passed down by the local veterans Catton grew up around in his boyhood home of Benzonia.

First person accounts such as those written by mid-Michigan authors **Sarah Emma Edmonds** who enlisted in the army as Franklin Thompson and **General James Harvey Kidd** who wrote about his service with General Custer and the Michigan Cavalry Brigade provide us with valuable insider information of the hardships and triumphs faced by the people of this era both on the home front and battlefield.

It was from the counties in mid and northern Michigan where Native Americans, who were not even United States citizens, joined the fray and fought courageously alongside their American brothers and sisters with one common purpose - to preserve and protect the Union.

Alma

RIVERSIDE CEMETERY
800 Washington Street

Brigadier General Ralph Ely, colonel of the 8th Michigan Infantry, is buried in Riverside Cemetery. He fought with his regiment in many major battles including Antietam, Fredericksburg, Vicksburg, Wilderness, Spotsylvania and Petersburg.

Bay City

HISTORICAL MUSEUM OF BAY COUNTY
321 Washington Avenue | (989) 893-5733
Civil War artifacts are on display.

BAY COUNTY WAR MEMORIAL
515 Center Avenue
Standing in front of the county building, the memorial lists the names of county soldiers who have died in the nation's wars, including the Civil War.

ELM LAWN CEMETERY

300 Ridge Road

Brigadier General Benjamin Franklin Partridge, who enlisted in the 16th Michigan as a 1st lieutenant and rose through the ranks to become regimental colonel, is interred here. He was wounded twice in battle.

PINE RIDGE CEMETERY

SE corner of Ridge and Tuscola Roads

An abandoned pioneer burial ground, Pine Ridge is the final resting place for many of Bay City's earliest pioneers. The cemetery was founded by **Judge James Birney**, an abolitionist who served as Lieutenant Governor of Michigan in 1861. Judge Birney, the brother of Major General David Birney of Pennsylvania, is also interred here.

The cemetery includes a Soldiers Rest, an area once maintained by the Grand Army of the Republic, Post #67 and burial sites for 150 Civil War veterans. A monument made of Whitney granite was erected by the local GAR Posts. Its inscription reads: "They saved their country And fought for freedom. They are quietly sleeping Under the 'Red, White and Blue' to preserve and strengthen those kind and fraternal feelings which bind together the soldiers and sailors of the rebellion."

Benzonia

BENZONIA TOWNSHIP CEMETERY

Love Road

Michigan's **Bruce Catton** (1899-1978) is best known for his two Civil War trilogies: *The Army of the Potomac* and *The Centennial History of the Civil War*. The historian, author and editor was born in Petoskey, but spent most of his childhood in Benzonia. At the age of fifty-one, after careers in the navy, journalism, and the federal government, Catton published his first Civil War Book, *Mr. Lincoln's Army*. In 1954 he became the editor of *American Heritage* magazine and was awarded the Pulitzer Prize for *A Stillness at Appomattox*. In 1978, Catton died at his Frankfort, Michigan, summer home.

Catton attributed his fascination with the Civil War to growing up with the Civil War veterans in Benzonia. The veterans, said Catton, "gave a color and a tone, not merely to our village life, but to the concept of life with which we grew up."

In the 1970s, Catton turned to his native state for inspiration and wrote: *Waiting for the Morning Train*, an account of his Michigan boyhood, and *Michigan: A Bicentennial History*.

BENZONIA AREA HISTORICAL MUSEUM

6941 Traverse Avenue | (231) 882-5539

Several Exhibits highlighting the life and accomplishments of author Bruce Catton can be found here.

MILLS COMMUNITY HOUSE

841 Michigan Avenue (U.S.-31)

A state historical marker denotes the former Benzonia Academy where historian and author **Bruce Catton** resided with his family after his father accepted a teaching position there. In 1906, Catton's father became the academy's principal. The Cattons lived in this building, which served as the principal's home and the female dormitory.

Big Rapids

HIGHLAND VIEW CEMETERY

607 West Bellevue Street

Brigadier Generals Stephen Bronson and **Joseph O. Hudnutt** are buried here. General Bronson joined the 12th Illinois Cavalry as a private and fought in the Battle of Gettysburg. He was appointed colonel of the 153rd Illinois Infantry and then brigadier general commanding the 1st Brigade of the Division of Western Tennessee. The lieutenant colonel of the 38th Iowa Infantry, Hudnutt was brevetted a brigadier general for faithful and meritorious service in the war.

CIVIL WAR SOLDIER MONUMENT

Southeast Corner of Stewart and Elm Streets

Erected by the Women of Mecosta County and dedicated in 1893, this monument depicting a lone soldier bearing a flag stands proudly in front of the Mecosta County Building.

Corunna

SHIAWASSEE COUNTY COURTHOUSE

208 N. Shiawassee Street

On the grounds of this beautiful and historic courthouse designed by Claire Allen stands an unusual Civil War monument with large draped American flags, similar in style to General Sherman's grave marker found at Calvary Cemetery in St. Louis, Missouri.

Flint

AVENTINE CEMETERY

Chavez Drive and Geneseret Street

A recently dedicated historical marker denotes Camp Thomson, the training site of the 10th Michigan Infantry from November 1, 1861 to April 22, 1862.

GENESEE COUNTY COURTHOUSE

900 South Saginaw Street

State historic marker pays tribute to Flint resident **Sarah Emma Edmonds** who enlisted in the Union Army on May 25, 1861, under the name of **Franklin Thompson**. Fearing her abusive father, the Canadian-born Edmonds, fled New Brunswick and settled in Flint where she sold books, disguised as a male, until entering the army. Two 30-pound Parrot rifled cannons are also located here as well as a monument to the GAR Crapo Post #145.

FINAL TWO SURVIVING CIVIL WAR VETERANS - The last two surviving Civil War veterans living in Michigan were Privates Orlando LeValley and Joseph Clovese. Private LeValley, a member of the 23rd Michigan Infantry, died on April 19, 1948 at age 99. He was the last surviving Civil War soldier from Michigan and is buried in Fairgrove's Brookside Cemetery. A granite monument was recently dedicated in his honor. Clovese, is not only the state's last surviving Civil War veteran, but he's also the last surviving black soldier in the Union Army. Born into slavery on a plantation in St. Bernard Parrish, Louisiana. Clovese escaped in his early teens and joined the Union Army. He became a member of the 63rd United States Colored Infantry who were recruited out of Louisiana. Near the end of his life, Clovese moved to Pontiac to be near family. He died on July 13, 1951 at age 107, while a patient at the former veteran's hospital in Dearborn. He is buried in Pontiac's Perry Mount Cemetery.

GLENWOOD CEMETERY

2500 West Court Street

Governor Henry H. Crapo, Michigan's 14th governor serving from January 1865 to January 1869 during the latter part of the Civil War and early years of Reconstruction, is interred here. **Brigadier General William Hawley**, colonel of the 3rd Wisconsin Infantry, is also buried here. General Hawley was with Sherman's army during the "March to the Sea." Confederate **Colonel George Dias**, Assistant Adjutant General on the staff of General Robert E. Lee, is buried here. He is the brother-in-law of famous Confederate General James Longstreet, also known as "Lee's old war horse."

Frankenmuth

MICHIGAN'S OWN MILITARY AND SPACE MUSEUM

1250 Weiss Street | (989) 652-8005 | admission fee

The largest collection of Medals of Honor in the entire nation are displayed here, including those belonging to Civil War heroes **General Thomas Withington** and **Thomas Bourne**.

Grayling

HARTWICK PINES STATE PARK

I-75 (exit 259) and M-93 | (989) 348-7608

Interpretative displays tell the history of Michigan's logging industry in the 1800s and the white pine forests of Michigan that covered a large part of the state during that period. Lumber, along with farming, iron, and copper, were the main industries in Michigan at the time of the Civil War. These industries played an integral role in Union success as they provided the raw materials necessary to produce weapons, ammunition and other much needed supplies.

Hart

OCEANA COUNTY COURTHOUSE

100 State Street

A detailed Civil War soldier monument stands on the front courthouse lawn.

Ionia

HIGHLAND PARK CEMETERY

East Main Street

This cemetery is the final resting place of **Brigadier General James Harvey Kidd**. General Kidd rose in rank to become colonel of the 6th Michigan Cavalry by recommendation of his commanding officer, General George A. Custer. He was brevetted brigadier general for gallant and meritorious service in the Shenandoah Valley campaign. General Kidd would also command the Michigan Cavalry Brigade. Later in life, General Kidd published his memoirs: *Recollections of a Cavalryman With Custer's Michigan Cavalry Brigade in the Civil War.*

IONIA COUNTY COURTHOUSE

100 West Main Street | (616) 527-5322

The regimental flag of the 21st Michigan Infantry, with separate battle honors banner, is displayed in all its glory on the first floor. The 21st trained at Camp Sigel which was located near here. On the courthouse grounds stands a unique Civil War soldier monument depicting the soldier's thumb on the hammer of his rifled musket getting "ready to fire."

CAMP SIGEL BOULDER AND PLAQUE

East Main Street

The 21st Michigan Infantry trained and organized at Ionia (Prairie Creek) in 1862. They would go on to fight at Perryville, Chickamauga, the Atlanta Campaign, Sherman's "March to the Sea" and the Carolinas.

Camp Sigel was the training ground of the 21st Michigan Infantry. The tablet was dedicated on September 12, 1912, to commemorate the fiftieth anniversary of the regiment's departure for the South, by the citizens of Ionia and surviving members of the regiment.

Ithaca

ITHACA CEMETERY

Spring and West North Streets

In this cemetery lies **Lieutenant Colonel Nathan Church** of the 26th Michigan Infantry whom General Nelson Miles called, "one of the best soldiers in the Army of the Potomac." On May 12, 1864, at the Battle of Spotsylvania Court House, Virginia, Church was one of the first soldiers to enter the Confederate works and engage in hand-to-hand combat at the "Bloody Angle". He was cited for gallery at Petersburg and for the Appomattox Campaign.

When the war ended, Church became Assistant Adjutant General on General Miles staff at Fortress Monroe where he oversaw the imprisonment of former Confederate President, Jefferson Davis.

Kalkaska

EVERGREEN CEMETERY

209 Laurel Street

Two Medal of Honor recipients from the same regiment, the 1st Michigan Sharpshooters, lie in rest at Evergreen Cemetery. **Sergeant Charles H. DePuy** was awarded his medal for aiding General Bartlett in working the guns in battle at Petersburg, Virginia, on July 30, 1864. **Private Charles M. Thatcher** was awarded his medal for actions on July 30, 1864, as well for not retreating or surrendering when the works was captured. Without regard for his own personal safety, Private Thatcher continued to return enemy fire.

Manistee

MANISTEE COUNTY HISTORICAL MUSEUM

425 River Street | (231) 723-5531

Civil War memorabilia exhibited here.

OAK GROVE CEMETERY

330 5th Street

Interred here is Medal of Honor recipient, **John Hyland**, an assistant gunner on the Navy ship USS Signal. Hyland was awarded the medal for his courageous actions on the Red River on May 5, 1864. Although wounded, he attempted to save his vessel while in full view of hundreds of Confederate sharpshooters.

Midland

NORTHWOOD UNIVERSITY CAMPUS

4000 Whiting Drive | behind Jordan Hall

A statue behind Jordan Hall depicts a young **Abe Lincoln** on horseback.

Muskegon

CIVIL WAR GENERAL STATUE

Peck and Terrace Streets

This statue pays tribute to **Major General Philip Kearny Jr.** who was killed at the Battle of Chantilly, Virginia on September 1, 1862.

HACKLEY PARK

West Clay Avenue and Third Street

An impressive 80-foot tall Civil War soldier's monument commands center stage in Hackley Park. Above and around the base, four bronze soldiers depict Civil

War military: infantry, cavalry, artillery and navy. Flanking the four corners of the park are commemorative statues of Admiral Farragut, General Sherman, General Grant and President Lincoln. A monument also pays tribute to William McKinley, a Civil War veteran and our nation's 25th President.

EVERGREEN CEMETERY

Irwin Avenue and Pine Street

Captain Jonathan Walker, a fishing boat captain who was caught trying to help seven slaves escape from Florida, is buried here. A Florida judge found Captain Walker guilty and sentenced him to one hour in the pillory, imprisonment, a fine and branding. The letters "SS" for slave stealer were branded onto his right hand. The outcry over what many deemed cruel punishment propelled Captain Walker into the national spotlight where he became a sought after speaker on the abolitionist speaking circuit and subject of the John Greenleaf Whittier poem: *The man with the Branded Hand*. A daguerreotype of Captain Walker's hand was made. Images reprinted from the daguerreotype were used in newspapers, abolitionist pamphlets, Walker's bestselling autobiography, and carved into the obelisk that marks his grave.

Petoskey

PETOSKEY DISTRICT LIBRARY CARNEGIE BUILDING

451 East Mitchell Street

Memorial stone pays tribute to historian and author **Bruce Catton** who was born in Petoskey on October 9, 1899. *(See Benzonia for more information on Bruce Catton).* Designed by local sculptor Stanley Kellogg, the stone with a bronze plaque depicting an image of the author was presented to the city in July of 1965.

LITTLE TRAVERSE HISTORY MUSEUM

100 Depot Court | (231) 347-2620

Exhibit dedicated to Bruce Catton can be found here.

Saginaw

BOULDER WITH BRONZE TABLET

Court Street and Washington Avenue

Boulder with bronze tablet marks the camp training site of the 23rd Michigan Infantry, utilized from August 10 to September 18, 1862.

BOULDER WITH BRONZE TABLET

North Michigan Avenue and Houghton Street

Boulder with bronze tablet marks the area where the 29th Michigan Infantry organized and trained from August 15 to October 6, 1864.

St. Johns

CLINTON COUNTY VETERANS MEMORIAL

Near Clinton Avenue and Railroad Street

This recently dedicated monument lists all Clinton County war dead including those from the Civil War and Medal of Honor recipients. Engraved on six of the ten tablets are the names of over 350 of Clinton County's "Boys in Blue" that never returned home.

MOUNT REST CEMETERY

600 North U.S.-Highway 27

Brigadier General Oliver Lyman Spaulding was commissioned a captain of the 23rd Michigan Infantry in 1862 and promoted to colonel of the regiment in 1864 is interred here. He was also a U.S. congressman. **Martha Brown Davis** is also buried here. She is the sister of the fiery and controversial abolitionist John Brown who was hanged for his armed occupation of the federal armory and arsenal at Harpers Ferry, Virginia in an attempt to raise a revolt against slavery.

A Civil War soldier monument at parade rest stands in remembrance within the cemetery.

OAK RIDGE CEMETERY

2518 S. Lowell Road

Medal of Honor recipient **Walter L. Mundell**, who enlisted in the 3rd Michigan Volunteer Infantry in 1861, lies in rest here. Before the Civil War's end, he served as a corporal in both the 3rd and 5th Michigan Volunteer Infantries and was wounded twice. On April 6, 1865, Corporal Mundell captured a Confederate battle flag at the Battle of Saylor's Creek, Virginia.

St. Louis

CIVIL WAR SOLDIER MONUMENT

M-46 and Michigan Avenue

A nice example of a traditional Civil War soldier monument at parade rest can be found here. Also, it is worth a trip to this picturesque small town just to say you have been to the middle of the mitten. St. Louis is the geographic center of Michigan's lower peninsula.

Traverse City

GRAND TRAVERSE COUNTY COURTHOUSE

Boardman and Washington Streets

Cannon and zinc Civil War soldier monument listing various battles around the base. The deteriorating monument was restored in 2005.

AUTHORS' TOP 10 MICHIGAN CIVIL WAR DESTINATIONS

1. *Annual Jackson "Civil War Muster" at Cascades Park*
2. *Monroe County Historical Museum in Monroe*
3. *Historic Fort Wayne in Detroit*
4. *Michigan Historical Museum/The Capitol in Lansing*
5. *Elmwood Cemetery in Detroit*
6. *Fort Wilkins at Copper Harbor*
7. *The Henry Ford in Dearborn*
8. *Fort Mackinac on Mackinac Island*
9. *Grand Rapids Museum in Grand Rapids*
10. *Copper Country in the Keweenaw Peninsula*

UPPER PENINSULA

4

*I*n addition to manpower, the Union relied heavily on the valuable natural resources found in Michigan's Upper Peninsula. The region supplied the military with two essential metals, copper and iron ore. At this time, copper could be found in almost everything from apparel to weapons. It was used to make the buttons and buckles on uniforms, as well as the bronze cannons used to repulse the enemy in the battlefield. Iron ore was crucial to the production of guns, cannon balls, cannons, railroad tracks, steam boilers and steel used to construct bridges.

These supplies were in high demand, therefore, massive quantities of copper and iron ore were mined to fulfill the ongoing need. If the North did not have access to these vital mines, the outcome of the Civil War may have been different. Therefore, we cannot emphasize enough the importance these mines found in Michigan's Upper Peninsula - along with the miners themselves - played in the Union victory.

Calumet

LAKEVIEW CEMETERY

24090 Veteran's Memorial Highway

Civil War soldier monument at parade rest located here.

KEWEENAW NATIONAL HISTORICAL PARK

Red Jacket Road and Calumet Avenue | Highway 41

Park interpretation focuses on buildings and sites associated with the former Calumet & Hecla Copper Mining Company. Michigan was the number one provider of copper to the Union army.

Copper Harbor

FORT WILKINS STATE PARK

U.S.-Highway 41 | (906) 289-4215

Built in 1844 to keep the peace during the state's copper boom, Fort Wilkins is very well preserved and sits atop the northern most point in Michigan. Abandoned, then regarrisoned in the 1860s, Civil War veterans were sent to the fort after the war as part of their duty assignments.

DELAWARE COPPER MINE

U.S. Highway 41 | 12 miles south of Copper Harbor | (906) 289-4688

Used from 1847 to 1887, the mine was a major supplier of copper to the Union effort.

Hancock

QUINCY MINE AND HOIST

49750 U.S. Highway 41 | (906) 482-3101

Established in 1848, the Quincy Mining company flourished during the Civil War with the increased demand for copper used in munitions.

Houghton

COLLEGE AVENUE PARK

Emerald Street and College Avenue

Civil War marching soldier monument with musket on shoulder located here.

POST MILITARY CEMETERY

Garrison Road | Mackinac State Park | (248) 328-0386

A National Historic Landmark, burials in this cemetery likely date back to the mid-1820s with the possibility of even earlier internments. In addition to soldiers and their families, six civilians are buried here.

ST. ANNE'S CATHOLIC MISSION CEMETERY

6837 Huron Street | (906) 847-3507

Second Lieutenant Garrett A Graveraet, 1st Michigan Sharpshooters, Company K, is buried here. An artist, musician and teacher at L'Abre Croche (*the Crooked Tree*), Lieutenant Graveraet helped recruit Indians from northwest Michigan to enlist in the 1st Michigan Infantry, Company K. (*See Company K entry for more information on this company*). Due to his European and Native American ancestry, census and war reports referred to Lieutenant Graveraet as a "half-breed."

The only enlisted white man recruited into Company K was **Henry Graveraet, Jr.**, formerly the probate judge of Emmett County and the Lieutenant's 55 year old father. On May 12, 1864, Henry was killed at the battle of Spotsylvania Courthouse in Virginia. Lt. Graveraet carefully marked the grave and surrounding trees so that he

Mackinac Island

FORT MACKINAC

7029 Huron Road | (906) 847-3328

Three prominent financiers of the Confederacy were imprisoned here as political prisoners during the summer of 1863 . A plaque honors Union **Brigadier General Thomas Williams** of Detroit who commanded the fort from 1852 to 1856. **Major General John Pemberton**, a native of Pennsylvania, and the Confederate commander at Vicksburg, Mississippi, served here in the 1850s.

could later locate his father's grave and take the body to Michigan for a proper burial according to the memoirs of Major Edward J. Buckabee, the regiment's adjutant.

Sadly, the 23 year old lieutenant would not return to claim his father's body. He died on July 1, 1864, from complications resulting from an injury sustained in battle outside Petersburg, Virginia on June 17.

The bodies of father and son were transferred to this Mackinac Island Cemetery where a marker honors them today.

Marquette
MARQUETTE REGIONAL HISTORY CENTER
145 W. Spring Street | (906) 226-3571
Civil War artifacts and GAR memorabilia exhibited.

LAKESIDE PARK
South East Street
Boulder with bronze plaque commemorates the local GAR and Women's Relief Corps.

Munising
RUSSELL A. ALGER MONUMENT
William G. Mather High School | Elm Avenue and Chocolay Street
A bust monument pays tribute to Russell Alger - a Civil War major general, Michigan governor, United States senator and secretary of war, whom Alger County is named after.

1ST MICHIGAN SHARPSHOOTERS, COMPANY K
Native Americans residing in Michigan, especially members of the Ojibwa, Odawa, and Potawatomi nations, composed the unit known as Company K of the 1st Michigan Infantry.

In May 1861, the idea of mustering a Native American regiment from Michigan was proposed by George Copway, a Chippewa Indian and Methodist minister. Although he touted their suitability for warfare, a prejudiced mentality toward the Native Americans - most of whom were not American citizens - prevailed in the Michigan legislature, and the proposal was rejected.

With the war escalating, and the realization that the conflict would not be short, a desperate need for draftees emerged. Suddenly the value of American Indians as excellent marksmen and warriors became apparent and recruitment ensued.

The 1st Michigan Infantry, including Company K, drilled at Detroit's Fort Wayne. In August 1863, they departed Detroit to guard Confederate prisoners at Fort Douglas in Chicago. In March 1864, they received orders to join with the Ninth Corps under the command of General Ambrose Burnside in Annapolis, Maryland.

Fierce, unconventional fighters, they saw action at the Battle of the Wilderness, Spotsylvania Court House, Cold Harbor, Petersburg, the Battle of the Crater, Ream's Station, Peebles Farm and Hatcher's Run. Over 150 Native Americans served in Company K. More than half died from wounds or disease. Nearly every man suffered some type of wound in battle. The 1st Michigan Sharpshooters mustered out of service in Jackson, Michigan on August 7, 1865.

Negaunee

MICHIGAN IRON INDUSTRY MUSEUM

73 Forge Road | *(906) 457-7857*

Michigan's iron ore was critical to the Union army in the production of iron based products such as cannons. Exhibits document the mining industry's contribution to the war effort.

JACKSON MINE

Intersection of Business Route M-28 and Cornish Town Road

A designated Michigan State Historic Site and listed on the National Register of Historic Places, Jackson Mine was the first iron mine in the Lake Superior region. It's here that iron ore was first discovered, the first mining done, and the first iron manufactured from its ore.

Jackson Mine was one of only three iron mines operating at the start of the Civil War. The company declared its first dividend in 1862 as production soared to fulfill the war's need for iron. In fact, demand was so high that ten new companies had formed by 1864.

Sault St. Marie

SOO LOCKS

Visitor's Center open seasonally from mid-May to mid-October | *(906) 632-3366*

The largest of the Soo Locks is Poe Lock, named for its original designer and builder **Brigadier General Orlando Poe**, who is buried at Arlington Cemetery. General Poe commanded the 2nd Michigan Infantry as its colonel and then became Sherman's chief engineer during the Atlanta Campaign and the "March to the Sea." He died on October 2, 1895 from complications due to an accident that took place at the locks.

RIVERSIDE CEMETERY

3260 Riverside Drive

First Sergeant Stephen O'Neill of Company E, 7th U.S. Infantry, is buried here. The Medal of Honor recipient earned his medal for actions at Chancellorsville, Virginia on May 1, 1863, where he picked up the unit's colors and carried them through the rest of the battle after the flag bearer was shot down.

St. Ignace

FORT DE BUADE MUSEUM

334 N. State Street | *(906) 643-6627*

This museum features Civil War artifacts and a display on Company K of the 1st Michigan Sharpshooters, a regiment made up of resident Native American soldiers primarily Ottawa and Ojibwa.

ARMY OF THE POTOMAC CHIEF OF ARTILLERY MAJOR GENERAL HENRY J. HUNT was born in Detroit in 1819, and named after his uncle, who served as the city's second mayor. A West Point graduate, Hunt spent 34 years in the army. Known as a great artillery tactician and strategist of the Civil War, Hunt, along with two other authors, revised the Instructions for Field Artillery, the guide used by Union field artillerists during the war. On July 3, 1863, at the Battle of Gettysburg, his brilliant strategy in the use of Union artillery during Pickett's Charge helped turn the tide resulting in Union victory. He is buried at Soldiers Home Cemetery, Washington D.C.

CIVIL WAR SITES

Copper
Harbor

Calumet
Hancock

Houghton

Marquette

Negaunee

Munising

Sault Ste. Marie

St. Ignace

Mackinac Island

Petoskey

Traverse City

Kalkaska

Benzonia

Grayling

Manistee

Big Rapids

Midland

Bay City

Hart

St. Louis

Alma

Saginaw

Ithaca

Frankenmuth

Muskegon

Grand
Rapids

Lowell

Saranac

St. Johns

Ionia

Flint

Port Huron

Sunfield

Corunna

Armada

Lansing

East
Lansing

Holland

Pontiac

Bloomfield Hills

Mt. Clemens

Hastings

Mason

Allegan

Stockbridge

Dexter

Plymouth

Kalamazoo

Battle Creek

Ann Arbor

Detroit

Galesburg

Marshall

Albion

Jackson

Ypsilanti

Dearborn

Union City

Brooklyn

Milan

Grosse Ile

New
Buffalo

Dowagiac

Tecumseh

Monroe

Three
Rivers

Vandalia

Coldwater

Jonesville

Tipton

Dundee

Niles

Centreville

Allen

Hillsdale

Adrian

White
Pigeon

Sturgis

Hudson

Blissfield

Map provided for general reference only.

ADDENDUM

Monument locations (clockwise from top left): Dexter, Dowagiac, Three Rivers, Hillsdale, Jackson, and Ann Arbor.

REGIMENTS THAT MUSTERED, TRAINED AND ORGANIZED IN EASTERN MICHIGAN

REGIMENT	COMMUNITY
1st Infantry	*Detroit and Ann Arbor*
2nd Infantry	*Detroit*
4th Infantry	*Adrian*
5th Infantry	*Detroit*
7th infantry	*Monroe*
8th Infantry	*Detroit*
9th Infantry	*Detroit*
10th Infantry	*Flint*
14th Infantry	*Ypsilanti*
15th Infantry	*Monroe*
16th Infantry	*Detroit*
17th Infantry	*Detroit*
18th Infantry	*Hillsdale*
20th Infantry	*Jackson*
22nd Infantry	*Pontiac*
23rd Infantry	*East Saginaw*
24th Infantry	*Detroit*
26th Infantry	*Jackson*
27th Infantry	*Ypsilanti*
29th Infantry	*Saginaw*
30th Infantry	*Detroit*
102nd U.S. Colored Infantry	*Detroit*
1st Cavalry	*Detroit*
4th Cavalry	*Detroit*
5th Cavalry	*Detroit*
8th Cavalry	*Mt. Clemens*
Michigan Light Artillery:	
Battery H	*Monroe*
Battery I	*Detroit*
Battery M	*Mt. Clemens*
1st Michigan Sharpshooters	*Dearborn*
1st U.S. Sharpshooters:	
Companies C, I, K.	*Detroit*
2nd U.S. Sharpshooters:	
Company B	*Detroit*

REGIMENTS THAT MUSTERED, TRAINED AND ORGANIZED IN WESTERN MICHIGAN

REGIMENT	COMMUNITY
3rd Infantry	*Grand Rapids*
6th Infantry	*Kalamazoo*
11th Infantry	*White Pigeon & Jackson*
12th Infantry	*Niles*
13th Infantry	*Kalamazoo*
19th Infantry	*Dowagiac*
21st Infantry	*Ionia*
25th Infantry	*Kalamazoo*
28th Infantry	*Kalamazoo*
2nd Cavalry	*Grand Rapids*
3rd Cavalry	*Grand Rapids*
6th Cavalry	*Grand Rapids*
7th Cavalry	*Grand Rapids*
9th Cavalry	*Coldwater*
10th Cavalry	*Grand Rapids*
11th Cavalry	*Kalamazoo*
1st Michigan Light Artillery:	
Battery A	*Coldwater*
Battery B	*Grand Rapids*
Battery C	*Grand Rapids*
Battery D	*White Pigeon*
Battery E	*Marshall*
Battery F	*Coldwater*
Battery G	*Kalamazoo*
Battery K	*Grand Rapids*
Battery L	*Coldwater*
13th Battery	*Grand Rapids*
14th Battery	*Kalamazoo*
1st Michigan Engineers & Mechanics	*Marshall*

CIVIL WAR EQUESTRIAN STATUES - *While equestrian monuments are common in eastern states, they are rare in Michigan. With only a handful located throughout the entire state, the following three equestrian statues represent our nation's Civil War era: Monroe's General George Custer at Elm and Monroe Streets; Detroit's General Alpheus Williams on Belle Isle; Midland's Young Abraham Lincoln at Northwood University.*

PROMINENT CIVIL WAR MONUMENTS AND STATUES IN MICHIGAN (117)

TOWN	LOCATION	TYPE OF MONUMENT
Adrian	Monument Park	Memorial Column
Adrian	Historical Museum	Laura Haviland Statue
Algonac	Boardwalk Park	Parade Rest Soldier
Allegan	Courthouse Lawn	Standard Bearer Soldier with Drawn Sword
Allen	Allen Cemetery	Parade Rest Soldier
Allendale	Allenendale Community Park	Veterans Memorial
Ann Arbor	Forest Hill Cemetery	Parade Rest Soldier
Ann Arbor	Fairview Cemetery	Monument with Carved Eagle
Athens	Burr Oak Cemetery	Parade Rest Soldier
Battle Creek	Monument Square	Tall Soldiers & Sailors
Battle Creek	Monument Park	Sojourner Truth
Battle Creek	East Michigan Ave.	Underground Railroad Sculpture
Battle Creek	Oak Hill Cemetery	Cannon from the "Cumberland"
Big Rapids	Courthouse Lawn	Standard Bearer Soldier
Birmingham	Shain Park	Obelisk to Local Soldiers & Sailors
Blissfield	Pleasantview Cemetery	Columbiad Cannon
Calumet	Lakeview Cemetery	Parade Rest Soldier
Carson City	City Park	Parade Rest Soldier
Cassville	Downtown Park	Parade Rest Soldier
Cedar Springs	Cedar Springs Cemetery	Parade Rest Soldier
Centreville	Prairie River Cemetery	Soldier Gazing Over the Horizon
Charlotte	Courthouse Lawn	Two Cannons
Chelsea	Oak Grove Cemetery	Parade Rest Soldier
Coldwater	Loomis Park	Original Battery A Parrot Cannon
Coldwater	Loomis Park	Monument Honoring "Old Sam" the War Horse
Coldwater	Public Library	Parade Rest Soldier
Corunna	Courthouse Lawn	Unique Flag Draped Memorial
Detroit	Campus Martius Park	Soldiers & Sailors
Detroit	Belle Isle	Equestrian Statue of General Alpheus Williams
Detroit	Belle Isle	Soldier Honoring the GAR
Detroit	Public Library on Library St.	Abraham Lincoln Statue
Detroit	Grand Circus Park	Russell Alger Memorial
Detroit	Grand Circus Park	Hazen Pingree Statue
Dexter	Village Park	Parade Rest Soldier
Dowagiac	Burke Street Park	Individual Soldiers with Standard Bearer
Dundee	Village Triangle Park	Memorial Bandstand with Parrot Cannon
Eaton Rapids	GAR Park	Monument to the GAR and Cannons
Farmington	Memorial Park	Memorial to Area War Dead
Fenton	Oak Hill Cemetery	Parade Rest Soldier
Galesburg	Downtown Square	General William Shafter Bust

Grand Haven ..... *Lake Forest Cemetery* .... *Parade Rest Soldier*

Grand Rapids ..... *Park at Division & Monroe Aves*. . . *Tall Zinc Parade Rest Soldier*

Grand Rapids ..... *Soldiers Home Cemetery*. .... *Soldier with Bowed Head & Hat in Hand*

Grandville. ...... *Grandville Cemetery* .... *Parade Rest Soldier*

Grant. .... *Ashland Center Cemetery*. .... *Parade Rest Soldier*

Hart .... *Courthouse Lawn*. .... *Parade Rest Soldier*

Hastings .... *Tyden Park*. .... *Tall Parade Rest Soldier*

Hillsdale .... *Courthouse Lawn*. .... *Sultana Memorial*

Hillsdale .... *Hillsdale College*. .... *Life Size Abraham Lincoln Statue*

Hillsdale .... *Hillsdale College*. .... *Standard Bearer Honoring Student Soldiers*

Hillsdale .... *Oakgrove Cemetery*. .... *Parade Rest Soldier*

Holland. .... *Pilgrim Cemetery*. .... *Parade Rest Soldier*

Houghton. .... *Park at Emerald St. & College Ave*. . *Marching Soldier*

Howell. .... *Lakeview Cemetery*. .... *Parade Rest Soldier*

Ionia .... *Courthouse Lawn*. .... *Soldier Cocking Hammer on Gun*

Ironwood .... *Riverview Cemetery* .... *Parade Rest Soldier*

Jackson .... *Withington Park* .... *"In Defense of the Flag" Soldier Statue*

Jackson .... *Mount Evergreen Cemetery* .... *Laura Evans Soldier Memorial*

Kalamazoo. ...... *Bronson Park* .... *Cannon & Numerous Plaques*

Kalamazoo. ...... *Riverside Cemetery* .... *Parade Rest Soldier*

Lake Odessa. ...... *Lakeside Cemetery*. .... *Soldier in Loading Position*

Lansing. .... *State Capital Lawn*. .... *Governor Austin Blair*

Lansing. .... *State Capital Lawn*. .... *1st Michigan Sharpshooters*

Lansing. .... *State Capital Lawn*. .... *1st Michigan Engineers & Mechanics*

Lansing. .... *Mount Hope Cemetery*. .... *Carved Obelisk*

Leonidas .... *Leonidas Cemetery*. .... *Parade Rest Soldier*

Lowell. .... *Oakwood Cemetery*. .... *Parade Rest Soldier*

Ludington .... *Lakeside Cemetery*. .... *Parade Rest Soldier*

Manchester. ...... *Oak Grove Cemetery* .... *Parade Rest Soldier*

Memphis .... *Memphis Cemetery*. .... *Parade Rest Soldier*

Menominee. ...... *Riverside Cemetery* .... *Parade Rest Soldier*

Midland .... *Northwood University* .... *Young Abraham Lincoln on Horseback*

Milan .... *Marble Park Cemetery* .... *Parade Rest Soldier*

Milford .... *Oak Grove Cemetery* .... *Parade Rest Soldier*

Monroe .... *Monroe & Elm Streets* .... *Equestrian Statue of General George Custer*

Monroe .... *Soldiers & Sailors Park* .... *Monroe County Civil War Memorial*

Morenci. .... *Oak Grove Cemetery* .... *GAR Memorial with Two Cannons*

Muskegon .... *Hackley Park* .... *Tall Memorial with Individual Soldiers and Victory*

Muskegon .... *Hackley Park* .... *President Abraham Lincoln*

Muskegon .... *Hackley Park* .... *General Ulysses Grant*

Muskegon .... *Hackley Park* .... *General William Sherman*

Muskegon .... *Hackley Park* .... *Admiral David Farragut*

Muskegon . . . . Hackley Park . . . . President William McKinley

Muskegon . . . . Peck & Terrace Streets. . . . . General Philip Kearny

Napoleon . . . . Napoleon Cemetery . . . . Marble Obelisk

Otsego. . . . . Mountain Home Cemetery . . . . Parade Rest Soldier

Owosso. . . . . Oak Hill Cemetery. . . . . Parade Rest Soldier

Petersburg. . . . . Downtown Park. . . . . Parade Rest Soldier

Plymouth . . . . Veterans Park. . . . . Memorial to the Fallen Sons of Plymouth

Plymouth . . . . Veterans Park. . . . . Civil War Monument/Veterans Memorial

Pontiac. . . . . City Hall. Parade Rest Soldier

Port Huron. . . . . . . Pine Grove Park. . . . . Tall Individual Soldiers with Standard Bearer

Portland. . . . . Portland Cemetery . . . . Parade Rest Soldier

Quincy . . . . Lakeview Cemetery. . . . . Zinc Parade Rest Soldier

Richmond. . . . . Richmond Cemetery. . . . . Parade Rest Soldier

Rockford . . . . Memorial Park . . . . Parade Rest Soldier

Rochester . . . . Mount Avon Cemetery. . . . . Parade Rest Soldier

Saginaw . . . . Oakwood Cemetery. . . . . Parade Rest Soldier

Sand Lake . . . . Sand Lake Cemetery. . . . . Parade Rest Soldier

Scottville. . . . . Lakeview Cemetery. . . . . Parade Rest Soldier

Sharan Twp.. . . . . . Sharon Center Cemetery. . . . . Marble Column

Shelby . . . . Village Park. . . . . Parade Rest Soldier

Shepherd. . . . . Coe Twp. Cemetery . . . . Parade Rest Soldier

Springport. . . . . . . Springport Cemetery . . . . Parade Rest Soldier

St. Johns . . . . Near Public Library . . . . Clinton County Veterans Memorial

St. Johns . . . . Mount Rest Cemetery. . . . . Parade Rest Soldier

St. Joseph. . . . . City Park. Dahlgren Cannon

St. Louis . . . . M-46 & Michigan Ave. . . . . Parade Rest Soldier

Stockbridge . . . . . . Public Square . . . . Parade Rest Soldier

Tecumseh . . . . Brookside Cemetery. . . . . Parade Rest Soldier with Cannons

Three Rivers . . . . . . Bowman Park . . . . Tall Parade Rest Soldier

Tipton . . . . Franklin Cemetery. . . . . Flag Draped Obelisk

Traverse City . . . . . . Courthouse Lawn. . . . . Zinc Parade Rest Soldier

Union City. . . . . . . Next to Congregational Church . . . . . Parade Rest Soldier

Wacousta. . . . . Wacousta Village Cemetery . . . . Parade Rest Soldier

Williamston . . . . . . City Hall. Parade Rest Soldier

Ypsilanti . . . . Highland Cemetery . . . . Standard Bearer Soldier

CIVIL WAR MEDAL OF HONOR RECIPIENTS BURIED IN MICHIGAN (53)

RANK	NAME	REGIMENT	CEMETERY	TOWN
Private	Frederick Alber	17th MI Inf	Oregon Twp.	Columbiaville
Private	John G.K. Ayers	8th MO Inf.	Riverside	Three Rivers
Private	Frederick Ballen	47th OH Inf.	Carleton	Carleton
Captain	Charles L. Barrell	102nd US Colored .	Hooker	Wayland

Corporal	Francis A. Bishop	57th PA Inf.	Blanchard	Blanchard
Chief Quartermaster	Thomas Bourne	US Navy	Poe	Jones
Sergeant	Joseph E. Brandle	17th MI Inf.	Oak Grove	Coldwater
1st Sergeant	Ivers S. Calkin	2nd NY Cav.	Oak Grove	Montague
Corporal	George W. Clute	14th MI Inf.	Mount Morris	Mount Morris
Coxswain	Patrick Colbert	US Navy	Mount Elliott	Detroit
Corporal	Gabriel Cole	5th MI Cav.	Sherman Twp.	Tustin
Brigadier General	Byron M. Cutcheon	20th MI Inf.	Highland	Ypsilanti
1st Sergeant	Charles H. Depuy	1st MI SS	Evergreen	Kalkaska
2nd Lieutenant	Henry M. Fox	5th MI Cav.	Mottville	Mottville
Private	Samuel S. French	7th MI Inf.	Gilford	Gilford
Sergeant	Robert J. Gardner	34th MA Inf.	Wright	Gregory
1st Lieutenant	Cornelius M. Hadley	9th MI Cav.	Mount Hope	Litchfield
Corporal	Sidney Haight	1st MI SS	West Reading	Reading
Corporal	Addison J. Hodges	47th OH Inf.	Ogden Zion	Blissfield
1st Sergeant	Charles M. Holton	7th MI Cav.	Oak Hill	Battle Creek
Sergeant	Michael Hudson	US Marine Corps	Maple Hill	Charlotte
Assistant Gunner	John Hyland	US Navy	Oak Grove	Manistee
1st Lieutenant	Patrick Irwin	14th MI Inf.	Saint Thomas Catholic	Ann Arbor
Sergeant	Elisha J. Johns	113th IL Inf.	Plum Grove	Union
Sergeant	Joseph S. Keen	13th MI Inf.	Elmwood	Detroit
Sergeant	Daniel A Kelly	8th NY Cav.	Old Maplewood	Reading
Captain	Joseph B. Kemp	5th MI Inf.	Forest Hill	Ann Arbor
1st Sergeant	Henry Lewis	47th OH Inf.	Soop-Pleasantview	Belleville
Sergeant	Frederick A. Lyon	1st VT Cav.	Mount Evergreen	Jackson
Sergeant	Daniel McFall	17th MI Inf.	Rice	Cone (Milan)
Sergeant	John W. Menter	5th MI Inf.	Franklin	Franklin
Corporal	Benjamin Morse	3rd MI Inf.	Oakwood	Lowell
Corporal	Walter L. Mundell	5th MI Inf.	Oak Ridge	St. Johns
Corporal	Henry E. Nash	47th OH Inf.	Palmyra	Palmyra
Sergeant	Conrad Noll	20th MI Inf.	Forest Hill	Ann Arbor
1st Lieutenant	Elliot M. Norton	6th MI Cav.	Liberty	Alamo
2nd Lieutenant	John R. Norton	1st NY Cav.	Forest Home	Greenville
1st Sergeant	Stephen O'Neill	7th US Inf.	Riverside	Sault Ste. Marie
Sergeant	Henry C. Peters	47th OH Inf.	Riverside	South Rockwood
Sergeant	Henry E. Plant	14th MI Inf.	Nunica	Nunica
Assistant Surgeon	George E. Ranney	2nd MI Cav.	Mount Hope	Lansing
Captain	Edwin F. Savacool	1st NY Cav.	Elmwood	Detroit
Private	Phillipp Schlachter	73rd NY Inf.	Oak Lawn	Sturgis
Brigadier General	Frederick W. Swift	17th MI Inf.	Elmwood	Detroit
Private	Peter Sype	47th OH Inf.	Trinity Lutheran	Monroe
Private	Charles M. Thatcher	1st MI SS	Evergreen	Kalkaska

2nd Lieutenant	James W. Toban	9th MI Cav.	Saint Patrick Calvary.. Brighton
Sergeant	Edward Van Winkle	145th NY Inf.	Oak Hill ... Battle Creek
Captain	William G. Whitney	11th MI Inf.	Allen ... Allen
Ordinary Seaman	Franklin L. Wilcox	US Navy	Soldiers Home ... Grand Rapids
Sergeant	William H. Wilcox	9th NH Inf.	Lakeview ... South Haven
Brigadier General	William H. Withington	1st MI Inf.	Mount Evergreen ... Jackson
Sergeant	Alonzo Woodruff	1st US SS	Valley ... Luther

CIVIL WAR GENERALS BURIED IN MICHIGAN (73)

RANK	NAME	CEMETERY	TOWN
Brigadier General	George S. Acker	Riverside	Union City
Major General	Russell A. Alger	Elmwood	Detroit
Brigadier General	Charles Barnes	Leelanau Twp.	Northport
Major General	Henry Baxter	Sunset View	Jonesville
Brigadier General	William H. H. Beadle	Riverside	Albion
Brigadier General	Thorton F. Broadhead	Elmwood	Detroit
Brigadier General	Stephen Bronson	Highland View	Big Rapids
Brigadier General	Simeon B. Brown	Hillside	St. Clair
Brigadier General	Stephen G. Champlin	Fulton Street	Grand Rapids
Brigadier General	Henry L. Chipman	Elmwood	Detroit
Brigadier General	Henry B. Clitz	Elmwood (Memorial)	Detroit
Major General	Philip St. George Cooke	Elmwood	Detroit
Brigadier General	Joseph T. Copeland	Oak Hill	Pontiac
Brigadier General	Byron M. Cutcheon	Highland Park	Ypsilanti
Brigadier General	Charles V. DeLand	Mount Evergreen	Jackson
Major General	Gustavus A. De Russy	Elmwood	Detroit
Brigadier General	Christopher J. Dickerson	Oak Grove	Hillsdale
Brigadier General	William H. Dickey	Riverside	Hastings
Major General	Henry M. Duffield	Elmwood	Detroit
Brigadier General	Ralph Ely	Riverside	Alma
Major General	Clinton B. Fisk	Oak Grove	Coldwater
Brigadier General	Mark Flanigan	Elmwood	Detroit
Brigadier General	William S. Green	Elmwood	Detroit
Brigadier General	Albert Hartsuff	Elmwood	Detroit
Brigadier General	William Hartsuff	Lakeside	Port Huron
Brigadier General	William Hawley	Glenwood	Flint
Brigadier General	Moses B. Houghton	Burdell Twp.	Tustin
Brigadier General	Joseph O. Hudnutt	Highland View	Big Rapids
Brigadier General	William Humphrey	Oakwood	Adrian
Brigadier General	Frederick S. Hutchinson	Soldiers Home	Grand Rapids
Brigadier General	William P. Innes	Fulton Street	Grand Rapids
Brigadier General	James H. Kidd	Highland Park	Ionia

Brigadier General	*Benjamin C. Lockwood*	*Elmwood*	*Detroit*
Brigadier General	*Cyrus O. Loomis*	*Elmwood*	*Detroit*
Brigadier General	*Salmon S. Matthews*	*Oak Hill*	*Pontiac*
Brigadier General	*Dwight May*	*Mountain Home*	*Kalamazoo*
Brigadier General	*Justus McKinstry*	*Highland Park*	*Ypsilanti*
Brigadier General	*Elisha Mix*	*Oakwood*	*Allegan*
Brigadier General	*Henry R. Mizner*	*Elmwood*	*Detroit*
Major General	*Henry A. Morrow*	*Silverbrook*	*Niles*
Quartermaster Gen.	*Friend Palmer*	*Elmwood*	*Detroit*
Brigadier General	*John G. Parkhurst*	*Oak Grove*	*Coldwater*
Brigadier General	*Benjamin F. Partridge*	*Elm Lawn*	*Bay City*
Major General	*Byron R. Pierce*	*Fulton Street*	*Grand Rapids*
Brigadier General	*James E. Pittman Jr.*	*Elmwood*	*Detroit*
Brigadier General	*Andrew Porter*	*Elmwood*	*Detroit*
Brigadier General	*Benjamin D. Pritchard*	*Oakwood*	*Allegan*
Brigadier General	*John Pulford*	*Elmwood*	*Detroit*
Major General	*Israel B. Richardson*	*Oak Hill*	*Pontiac*
Brigadier General	*Eugene Robinson*	*Elmwood*	*Detroit*
Brigadier General	*John Robertson*	*Elmwood*	*Detroit*
Brigadier General	*William Sanborn*	*Lakeside*	*Port Huron*
Brigadier General	*George T. Shaffer*	*Shaffer*	*Cassopolis*
Brigadier General	*Jacob Sharpe*	*Elmwood*	*Detroit*
Brigadier General	*Charles E. Smith*	*Mountain Home*	*Kalamazoo*
Brigadier General	*Israel C. Smith*	*Oakhill*	*Grand Rapids*
Brigadier General	*Joseph R. Smith*	*Woodland*	*Monroe*
Brigadier General	*George Spalding*	*Woodland*	*Monroe*
Brigadier General	*Oliver L. Spaulding*	*Mount Rest*	*St. Johns*
Brigadier General	*Ambrose A. Stevens*	*Saranac*	*Saranac*
Major General	*William L. Stoughton*	*Oak Lawn*	*Sturgis*
Brigadier General	*David Stuart*	*Elmwood*	*Detroit*
Brigadier General	*Frederick W. Swift*	*Elmwood*	*Detroit*
Brigadier General	*Henry D. Terry*	*Clinton Grove*	*Mt. Clemens*
Brigadier General	*William A. Throop*	*Elmwood*	*Detroit*
Brigadier General	*Charles S. Tripler*	*Elmwood*	*Detroit*
Major General	*Luther S. Trowbridge*	*Elmwood*	*Detroit*
Brigadier General	*Michael J. Vreeland*	*Woodmere*	*Detroit*
Brigadier General	*Lyman M. Ward*	*Crystal Springs*	*Benton Harbor*
Major General	*Alpheus S. Williams*	*Elmwood*	*Detroit*
Brigadier General	*Thomas R. Williams*	*Elmwood*	*Detroit*
Brigadier General	*William H. Withington*	*Mount Evergreen*	*Jackson*
Brigadier General	*Grover S. Wormer*	*Elmwood*	*Detroit*

SOURCES | SUGGESTED READINGS

Adjutant General of Michigan. *Record of Service of Michigan Volunteers in the Civil War, 1861-1865.* Kalamazoo: Ihling Brothers and Everand, 1905.

"African Americans in the Civil War." *The Mitten.* December 2002.

Anderson, Loraine. "Two Northern Michigan Men, Two Destinies." *Traverse City Record-Eagle* 22 Feb. 2009.

Anderson, William M. *They Died to Make Men Free: The History of the 19th Michigan Infantry in the Civil War.* Dayton: Morningside House, Inc., 1994.

Bak, Richard. *A Distant Thunder: Michigan in the Civil War.* Ann Arbor, MI: Huron River Press, 2004.

Baut, Donald V. "The Detroit Arsenal Story, 1833-1875." *The Dearborn Historian* 17 Winter 1977: 23-29.

Bertera, Martin and Kim Crawford. *The 4th Michigan Infantry and the Civil War.* East Lansing: Michigan State Press, 2010.

Bitter, Rand K. *Minty and His Cavalry: A History of the Saber Brigade and its Commander.* Self, 2006.

Bozich, Stanley J. *Michigan's Own: The Medal of Honor, Civil War to Vietnam War.* Frankenmuth, MI: Polar Bear Publishing, 1987.

Chartkoff, Kerry. "Civil War 150th Anniversary: Michigan in the Civil War 1861 – 1865." 2011.

Conway, James and David Jamroz. *Detroit's Historic Fort Wayne.* Mount Pleasant, SC: Arcadia Publishing, 2007.

Curtis, Orson. *History of the 24th Michigan of the Iron Brigade, Known as the Detroit and Wayne County Regiment.* Gathersburg, MD: Old Soldier Books, Inc., 1988.

Dempsey, Jack. *Michigan and the Civil War: A Great and Bloody Sacrifice.* Charleston, SC: The History Press, 2011.

Frank, Michael S. *Elmwood Endures: History of a Detroit Cemetery.* Detroit: Wayne State University Press, 1996.

Garrett, Bob. "Flight to Freedom." *Seeking Michigan.* 2 Feb. 2010 < seekingmichigan.org/look/2010/02/02/crosswhite" http://seekingmichigan.org/look/2010/02/02/crosswhite>

Herek, Raymond. *These Men Have Seen Hard Service: The First Michigan Sharpshooters in the Civil War.* Detroit: Great Lakes Books, 1998.

Hershenzon, Gail D. *Images of America: Detroit's Woodmere Cemetery.* Mount Pleasant, SC: Arcadia Publishing, 2006.

Hoffman, Mark. *My Brave Mechanics: The First Michigan Engineers and Their Civil War.* Detroit: Wayne State University Press, 2007.

Hunt, Roger D. *Colonels in Blue: Michigan, Ohio and West Virginia.* Jefferson, NC: McFarland and Company, 2011.

Hunt, Roger D. and Jack R. Brown. *Brevet Brigadier Generals in Blue.* Gaithersburg, MD: Olde Soldiers Books, Inc., 1997.

Kidd, James. *Riding With Custer: Recollections of a Cavalryman in the Civil War.* Lincoln: University of Nebraska Press, 1997.

Kundinger, Matthew. "Racial Rhetoric: The Detroit Free Press and Its Part in the Detroit Race Riot of 1863." *Michigan Journal of History,* 2006.

Longacre, Edward. *Custer and his Wolverines: The Michigan Cavalry Brigade, 1861-1865.* Conshohocken, PA: Combined Publishing, 1997.

Mason, Jack C. *Until Antietam: The Life and Letters of Major General Israel B. Richardson, U.S. Army.* Charbondale: Southern Illinois University Press, 2009.

Mason, Philip and Paul Pentecost. *From Bull Run to Appomattox: Michigan's Role in the Civil War.* Detroit: Wayne State University Press, 1961.

May, George. *Michigan and the Civil War Years, 1860-1866: A War Time Chronicle.* Lansing: Michigan Civil War Centennial Observance Commission, 1964.

May, George. *Michigan Civil War Monuments*. Lansing: Michigan Civil War Centennial Observance Commission, 1965.

McCarthy, Bernard and Chancey P. Miller, Joseph R. Schroeder. *The Civil War Veterans*. Detroit: Elmwood Cemetery, 1993.

Michigan and the Civil War: An Anthology. Michigan History Magazine 1999.

"Michigan Notables and Civil War Soldiers Buried at Woodmere Cemetery." Woodmere Cemetery.

Millbrook, Minnie. *A Study in Valor: Michigan Medal of Honor Winners in the Civil War*. Lansing: Michigan Civil War Centennial Observance Commission, 1966.

Millbrook, Minnie. *Twice Told Tales of Michigan and Her Soldiers in the Civil War*. Lansing: Michigan Civil War Centennial Observance Commission, 1966.

Miller, Chancey P. *The Civil War Generals*. Detroit: Elmwood Cemetery.

Panhorst, Michael W. "Outdoor Sculpture in Jackson, Michigan. 2006. *Ella Sharp Musuem* ‹www.ellasharp.org/our-outdoor-sculpture.html" http://www.ellasharp.org/our-outdoor-sculpture.html›

Petz, Weldon E. and Roger Rosentreter. *Seeking Lincoln in Michigan*. Michigan History Magazine 2009.

Quaife, Milo M., Ed. *From the Cannon's Mouth: The Civil War of General Alpheus S. Williams*. Detroit: Wayne State University Press, 1959.

Robertson, John. *Michigan in the War*. Lansing: W.S. George and Co., 1882.

Scott, Robert, Ed. *Forgotten Valor: The Memoirs, Journals and Civil War Letters of Orlando B. Willcox*. Kent: The Kent State University Press, 1999.

Sheppard, Lawrence C. "A Tale of the 'Old Flag.'" *The Dearborn Historian* 18 Autumn 1978: 108-111.

Stoy, Roland. "Famous Horse Subject of Local Publication." *The Daily Reporter* 2009.

Thank God for Michigan: Civil War Collector's Issue. Michigan History Magazine, 1998.

"The Raid on Harpers Ferry." *Africans in America PBS People and Events* 1859 www.pbs.org/wgbh/aia/part4/4p2940.html" http://www.pbs.org/wgbh/aia/part4/4p2940.html›

Thornton, Leland W. *When Gallantry Was Commonplace: The History of the Michigan Eleventh Volunteer Infantry, 1861-1864*. American University Studies Series 9, Vol. 90. New York: P. Lang, 1991.

Townsend, David G. *The Seventh Michigan Volunteer Infantry: The Gallant Men and Flag in the Civil War, 1861-1865*. Fort Lauderdale, FL: Southeast Publications, 1993.

Urwin, Gregory. *Custer Victorious: The Civil War Battles of General George Armstrong Custer*. Lincoln: University of Nebraska Press, 1983.

Warren, Ezra J. *Generals in Blue*. Baton Rouge: Louisiana State University Press, 1992.

Williams, Frederick. *Michigan Soldiers in the Civil War*. Lansing: Michigan Historical Commission, 2002.

Woodford, Frank. *Father Abraham's Children: Michigan Episodes in the Civil War*. Detroit: Wayne State University Press, 1961.

Woodford, Frank B. and Arthur M. Woodford. *All Our Yesterdays: A Brief History of Detroit*. Wayne State University Press, 1969.

Wunderlich, Kevin D. *Images of America: Vernor's Ginger Ale*. Mt. Pleasant, SC: Arcadia Publishing, 2008.

WEBSITES: *4thmichigan.com | 7thmichigan.us | aadl.org | awesometalks.wordpress.com | cia.gov | civilwar.org civilwararchive.com/unionmi.htm | detroit1701.org | findagrave.com | generalsandbrevets.com harriettubmanbiography.com | historicfortwaynecoalition.com | hmdb.org | homeofheroes.com hometownhistorytours.com | itd.nps.gov/cwss | michiganinthewar.org | michiganmarkers.com nps.org | roadsandriders.com/memorials/mi/index.html | seekingmichigan.org/civilwar thehenryford.com | wayfinder.com | wikipedia.com*

INDEX

About the Authors

Karin Risko

"You could say the idea for Hometown History Tours and this guidebook originated way back in elementary school when my family moved to Lincoln Park. Eager to show my older sisters and me around, the neighborhood kids invited us to come see the Indian Stone dedicated to Chief Pontiac.

As we made the three or four block walk, I was really excited. Although I had no clue who Chief Pontiac was and didn't know anything about his famous council or the Siege of Detroit, I was awestruck that something this big had happened nearby to warrant a marker. Once we arrived at the stone, I was flabbergasted that no other people were lined up waiting to see this amazing piece of history.

The sense of amazement I felt when I first saw the Indian Stone has stayed with me throughout my life and flares up whenever I come across information that ties our local history to national events. To me, these ties bring history alive and make it so much more interesting. It's my hope that you too will be amazed by all the important history that surrounds you."

– Karin Risko, founder and director of Hometown History Tours
(A former history teacher, Karin earned a bachelor's degree from Central Michigan University.)

David Ingall

A resident of Temperance, Michigan, David Ingall has visited almost every major Civil War battlefield in the nation - many numerous times. He's conducted exhaustive research on the soldiers from Monroe County including his own 20 relatives who fought in the Civil War. He's also an expert on General George Armstrong Custer, the Union Civil War hero who made Monroe, Michigan his adopted hometown. The former assistant director at the Monroe County Historical Museum, home to the largest Custer collection in the world, Dave presented the General's story to museum visitors from around the world.

The War of 1812, particularly the local Battle of the River Raisin - one of the war's bloodiest battles – is another of Dave's favorite topics. A former interpreter at the Monroe battlefield site, now a National Park, Dave lead many tours and has been called upon numerous times to give presentations on the battle before many groups.

A member of several historic and preservation organizations, Dave's knowledge of and passion for history make him a sought after speaker by Civil War Round Tables as well as educational and historical organizations. He's also a popular tour guide for Hometown History Tours.
(Dave holds a bachelor's degree from Western Michigan University.)